# What readers are saying about
# Empower your Voice

"Any woman, any age who feels she has something worth saying but that no one is listening needs Rena Cook's *Empower Your Voice...*" Powerful, practical, intimate and honest, Cook addresses our sabotaging fears with kick-ass courage and solid solutions. Not since Julia Cameron's *Artist's Way* initiative have I come upon such an accessible, challenging and effective approach to self -realization."

   -Sheila Rinear, Playwright/ Screenwriter and Educator

"After almost a decade of training women to run for political office, Rena Cook's book is a welcome addition to our tool box. While we are experienced at helping a female candidate hone her message, our expertise stopped at the delivery; voice preparation, vocal tone, rhythm of speech. *Empower Your Voice* fills the void. As Rena points out, likability of a person is often based on the first few words out of her mouth. Anyone who reads this book and practices the exercises within will raise her potential for likability a hundredfold. For candidates and non-candidates alike, *Empower Your Voice* is a must."

   -Sara Jane Rose, Interim Executive Director

"I have been speaking in public professionally my entire adult life. Rena helped me figure out how to find my authentic voice. The exercises and instructions in this book lay out the methods Rena used in person. The illustrations and videos show how to implement these exercises properly. Following these methods and practicing them will help other women find their authentic voice also."

   -Laurie Koller, Attorney

# Empower your Voice:
# For Women in Business,
# Politics and Life

### Rena Cook

www.TotalPublishingAndMedia.com

Photo credits
Front Cover: Markeida Johnson, Jade Latimer Graham, Kendra Horn, Cecilia Wessinger, Estela Hernandez, Melanie Fry, Shay White, Alissa Mortimer

Back Cover: Estela Hernandez, Melanie Fry, Shay White, Rena Cook, Diana Morgan, Markeida Johnson, Jade Latimer Graham

ISBN 978-1-63302-086-3

Illustrated by Carey Hissey

Video produced by Inspyred Images
Deana Spyres and Don Kreutzweiser

Cover and Internal Photographs by Don Kreutzweiser

Cover Design by Deana Spyres

Total Publishing and Media

# Table of Contents

# Acknowledgements

My mentors have deep pockets! Through the years, they have generously allowed me to dig deep into their pockets of wisdom and knowledge. Wherever I have been, inspiring and dedicated master teachers have been there before me, laying the foundation of this work. I humbly thank them here: David Carey, Jane Boston, Rocco Dal Vera, Paul Meier, Leslie-Ann Timlick, Gillyanne Keyes, Patsy Rodenburg, Kristin Linklater, Jack Wright, Ron Willis, John Gronbeck-Tedesco and Allan Sterrett.

Heartfelt thanks to:

Julie McCoy, Anna Fearheiley, Kim Moore and Pat Mitcho for editing and giving honest, informed feedback. Lauralee Dick who edits and solves formatting puzzles.

Matthew Ellis for his invaluable contribution to Chapter 9, "Communicating through Body Language."

Melanie Fry, Estela Hernandez, Kendra Horn, Markeida Johnson, Jade Latimer Graham, Diana Morgan, Alissa Mortimer, Cecilia Wessinger, Shay White, Erin Weaver, and Robin Rogers are the beautiful ladies on the cover, in photos and illustrations who have shared this work with me.

Teri Aulph, Angela Byers, Felicia Correia, Cecilie Croissant, Anna Fearheiley, Aurora Gregory, Kendra Horn, Ellen McClure, Diana Morgan, Cheena Pazzo, Jessica Reading and Kathy Taylor are a group of highly accomplished, dynamic and inspiring women who agreed to be interviewed for this book.

Their thoughts and wisdom appear in "Voices from the Field" at the end of each chapter.

Julie McCoy and Deonna Prince for appearing with me in the video.

Robert Johnson, founder of Bold Growth Strategies, for his deep understanding of entrepreneurial networking and the perfect 60-second pitch.

Tulsa Community College, Kelly Clark and Mark Frank

Oklahoma City University, Brian Parsons and D. Lance Marsh

Peter Biadasz, Total Publishing and Media.

James Bullis, MVP Startups.

Don Kreutzweiser and Deana Spyres, Inspyred Images: video, photography, and cover design.

Carey Hissy, illustrator extraordinaire, this is our second project together.

My husband Joe Mitcho who has always given me room to follow my dreams.

# Dedication

For my brother Lacy who first believed in me...and still does.

# Foreword

Several years ago, I was hired to work with a female client who was attempting to reach partner status at one of the "Big 5" accounting firms. She was a high performer who was recognized as an effective leader by her direct reports, peers and senior management. She also was an innovative contributor to the firm with a keen ability to recognize opportunities that both generated revenue and grew their client base. Despite all this, in her previous year's bid for partner, she'd been turned down. The question no one could answer was "why?" When asked for constructive feedback, the senior partners who were responsible for moving this talented woman's career forward could only answer, "We're not sure why. There is simply something about her that doesn't say 'leader'."

On our first meeting, as she walked into the room, I was struck by her presence. Confident and charismatic, she embodied the essence of a successful leader. The moment she spoke, I realized her challenge. While she exuded leadership in her non-verbal communication, her verbal communication was incongruent with her physical presentation. She spoke in an extremely high, breathy voice and was hesitant in her delivery. She turned statements into questions and inserted "um" several times in every sentence. As she spoke, she evoked an almost child-like presence that eroded the credibility she'd brought into the room.

When I suggested that her voice might be the primary blocker to her career advancement, she was shocked. How could something as simple as one's voice be the key issue to keeping her from having a "seat at the table?" I admitted it may not be the only blocker but asked if she'd be willing to try an experiment: work on her voice for six months to a year and see what happened. She agreed and went on to become a partner who is now a highly successful CFO at a major corporation.

As Rena Cook says in this book, "Our voice is the inner expression of who we are. It reflects our innermost sense of self and authenticity." It may not be the only thing that establishes us as leaders, but it could be the one thing that erodes our credibility and keeps us from being heard. *Empower Your Voice* is the first book of its kind to introduce an easy to follow, supportive and empowering methodology that helps women "find their voice," and release the most powerful and authentic expression of their leadership potential.

I have known and worked with Ms. Cook for nearly 20 years. She is a passionate and compassionate teacher whose work has been inspired by her own journey in discovering her authentic voice. This journey has led her to a deep understanding of the challenges we as women face – from daily overuse of our voices to being told we sound too harsh or abrasive or too much like a little girl. Rena's work is to help each and every female leader unlock a voice that is powerful, resonant and, most importantly, authentic.

More than ever before, we live in a time of tremendous leadership opportunity and challenges for women. For example, not-for-profit organizations that support female candidates say the numbers of women asking for training and support in running for election have more than doubled since January 2017. This increase is on both sides of the political spectrum. The Center for American Women and Politics, a non-partisan group that runs a "Ready to Run" yearly workshop for potential candidates, saw the number of delegates to this year's conference double.

Women have made great strides in moving into the upper echelons of power and influence, yet we still face numerous barriers to equal representation in the workforce, in government and beyond. While perceptions of women in leadership are changing, much work needs to be done to overcome limiting views and judgments about the role of women, our strength and capacity to lead. *Empower Your Voice* is an essential tool for any woman who is called to lead, who is moved to ignite change and is courageous enough to claim the challenge of leadership.

Whether you seek higher office, a seat at the board of directors table or a personal breakthrough, Ms. Cook invites you to explore, experiment, play and feel empowered to find your true voice. She uses her deep expertise to challenge you to step out of your comfort zone and find a voice, your voice, which truly represents your values, beliefs and convictions.

Jacqueline Farrington PCC
Organizational and Executive Coach, Change Communications Practitioner, TEDx Seattle speaker coach

Rena and Cecilia practice deep breathing techniques

# Introduction

"Creative expression and engagement are hot; stoicism and pontification are not. The feminine attributes of engaging in dialogue, listening, disclosing, being animated, and showing empathy - traditionally considered signs of weakness – are now valued and expected."
Christine K. Jahnke[1]

On January 21, 2017, I marched in Oklahoma City, while millions of other women around the world marched, raising our collective voices. A sea of women of all ages and ethnicities applauded the speeches of thought leaders, carried signs both serious and bitingly satirical and created a wave of hopeful, enthusiastic civic engagement. Now, more than ever, women are activated and energized, filled with thoughts, ambitions, opinions and dreams for positive change, for recognition, for equality, for our families, our neighbors, our communities, and our nation. We are making progress! Today more women lead cities, states, companies and countries than ever before. Hillary Clinton almost broke that highest of glass ceilings. Elizabeth Warren fearlessly speaks truth to power. Carly Fiorina clearly articulates complex information on national stages. In this last election cycle, we saw women representing multiple points of view, expressing opinions, voicing outrage and hope, giving us a unique opportunity to look closely at their various communication styles. As successful as these high profile women are, many sabotage themselves because they have not learned how to express themselves in a way that is authentic and engaging. Women in positions of leadership often receive feedback that they are harsh, shrill, and abrasive. Women wanting to move up the corporate ladder may receive feedback that they sound too young, apologetic or indecisive. Ineffective communication habits created over years, even decades, frequently obscure the message. Even as we are inspired to own our voices, self-defeating vocal habits can stop us in our tracks. How does a woman overcome physical and psychological habits so her voice conveys confidence, presence, and authentic power?

My consultancy business, Vocal Authority, is full of women who had been told, "You can't be heard, own your voice, find your voice, speak up!" Or just as commonly, "Tone it down, you are bossy, aggressive, shrill!" I have clients who say, "I need to find my voice. Nobody listens to me. I am not taken seriously." "I hate my voice." "My voice is just naturally soft." "People say I sound angry." "My voice is naturally loud, I can't help it."

As diverse as these issues seem, there is a common solution. Whether you press too hard or under-energize your voice, there is a path to a grounded, centered, confident voice that can be heard, respected and accepted. The women I encounter yearn to speak personal truth in all situations, whether they're speaking to leaders or are in leadership positions themselves. My first word of reassurance to these women is that it is easy to make significant changes in your voice. But real and lasting change takes time. If, for example, you decided you wanted to be a marathon runner, you know you would have to commit to weeks, even months, of deliberate practice. If you want to play the violin, you can't just read a book about the violin and expect to play music worthy of an audience. If you believe your voice has been holding you back from achieving your career goals, or if you are inspired to run for political office, you will hear and feel lasting changes when you commit to dedicated and focused vocal practice.

I came to this work through the theatre. I started life as a singer, actor, dancer. When I was five years old, I made potholders and sold them door to door to buy my first pair of tap shoes. You know the ones - black patent leather with grosgrain ribbons. I was in college, thinking I was bound for Broadway, when I directed a play and taught a class. It was like taking blinders off! I saw for the first time that performing was all about me, while teaching was all about us, what we could do together. I became a high school drama teacher dedicated to saving the world, one drama student at a time. I loved watching my students grow in confidence. Hearing them own their voices was the joy of my existence. Wanting to learn more about the theatre and grow as a teacher, I went back to school, got another degree and began to teach in higher education, training future professional actors.

As I taught, directed and coached actors, I began to understand that if the voice is not working, nothing else will work. So again I went back to school. I left my university job to attend London's Royal Central School of Speech and Drama where I earned a Master of Arts degree in Voice Studies. I returned to pick up my work in actor training with a huge new arsenal for developing the speaking voice. I spent another 15 years at the University of Oklahoma School of Drama working with amazing young actors, many of whom are now in New York City, Chicago and Los Angeles on stage, in film and on television. I relished this work for the deep sense of satisfaction I gained from knowing I was contributing to my students' ability to realize their dreams. My skills as a voice trainer grew as I became more and more certain that it is, indeed, all about the voice!

There was however always a niggling sense in the back of my mind: Could the techniques that I'd developed over the years helping actors to flourish vocally be used in business, legal and political settings? Thus Vocal Authority was born. Not surprisingly, the work I do with women has become the most energizing and deeply satisfying aspect of my teaching. Empowering women's voices is now my central mission with the goal of helping women find more powerful, authentic and expressive speaking voices.

I have observed, and my research has confirmed, as young girls reach the junior high years, they start hiding and denying their own voices in order to maintain relationships with their girlfriends, within the family and with boys (see chapter 1). Reflecting on my own vocal journey, I see that this happened to me and I can trace a pretty wild ride as I alternately hid my voice, or shared way too much of it. I then developed what I call situational vocal confidence. As a teacher, in my own classroom, I had a strong, expressive voice. But in faculty meetings, for example, I became quite good at denying the stronger sides of my nature - leading, speaking out, setting agenda - for fear that I would be labeled as "hard to work with." I developed a self-deprecating nature, content to play the professional peacemaker. Now that's not a bad role, I am proud of my skills in that area and they have served me well in numerous organizations. However, I was not viewed by colleagues as leaderly; they did not trust that I could have the difficult conversations or make the hard choices. Ultimately, through reflection and practice, I have emerged a more confident and grounded communicator. That is why, at this time in my life, I am compelled to offer a process to women who aspire to leadership roles in business and politics, which will empower their voices in real, tangible and permanent ways.

As I prepared to write this book, I read classic feminist tomes and contemporary books and articles on women's issues. There are many current books written for women by women concerning our professional challenges, all encouraging us to speak up, own our power, lean in, push back, take our place, take our seat, have confidence and be present and authentic. Many give inspiration, insights and understandings. The piece that I have found missing in most of these books is *how*. How exactly does a woman overcome years of habitual ways of using her voice to find a clear, strong voice that conveys confidence, presence and authentic power? We can intellectually understand a concept but not be able to make our bodies actually put it into practice. The clear and effective voice is made up of a series of bodily systems that must ultimately work in a natural synchronization, which is why vocal improvement has remained somewhat of a mystery. *Empower Your Voice: For Women in Business, Politics and Life* lays out a clear process for taking on new habits, working with our body's muscle memory to actually learn to speak in a new and more effective way. Real and lasting change comes through dedicated practice.

## Using this Book

Each chapter is organized around an aspect of the voice and contains descriptions, definitions and exercises. The book is laid out in a sequential fashion so it is best to work through the chapters as presented. If you're tempted to skip right to the chapter on Running for Political Office, for example, you will miss some vital information and foundational skill-based work that will insure success.

In this work, you will be active, on your feet, saying phrases, sentences and speeches out loud. I will frequently ask you to be "aware" of what you feel, notice or experience. Developing personal awareness is crucial as we change old habits for new ones.

You will be encouraged to write about what you experience and learn. I have provided a place to journal, along with prompts to stimulate deeper reflection and encourage consistent practice. The very act of putting experiences into writing deepens the lessons and helps new and more effective behaviors take root, grow and thrive.

The complimentary video is the "secret sauce." Go to my website www.myvocalauthority.com and type in the access code 50602Empower. Use it! You can do the vocal warm up with me every day. The women featured in the video have worked with me and will also model the work for you.

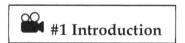
#1 Introduction

Quotations from leading authors and researchers introduce each chapter. I want to give readers a glimpse into what other successful business professionals are saying about women and voice.

I interviewed twelve successful women from across the country representing a wide range of fields - corporate, political, academic and entertainment. These amazing women gave me the gift of their time and open-heartedly shared their stories, reflections and advice about gender, voice, communication styles and their relationship to success. Their words place our work in a larger, real-world context. Their inspiring contributions are featured in "Voices from the Field," at the end of each chapter. A bio of each woman can be found at the end of the book.

Illustrator Carey Hissey, who worked with me on *Voice and the Young Actor,* has created timeless illustrations of women as they model various exercises described in the narrative.

The narrative and exercises in this book cover a wide range of topics, including

- Grounding and centering
- Releasing habitual tension
- Finding natural alignment
- Breathing deeply and centrally
- Managing performance anxiety, building confidence and presence
- Empowering resonance, opening the vocal tract and making space for sound
- Articulating with clarity and muscularity
- Using clear and meaningful body language to support your message
- Making speeches more dynamic and compelling

- Owning the room
- Running for office and managing the media

Find a buddy to go through this process with you. If you meet once a week and work through the exercises together, giving support, feedback and accountability, the vocal growth of each of you will soar. Form small groups of like-minded women and take each other through the work – it is all laid out for you to follow. A different member from the group could lead each week's session. Between the content outlined in the book and the video you have all the tools you need.

The act of writing this book has clarified and deepened my commitment to truly make a difference in the lives of women who have been silenced, held back, recently promoted or newly activated. All of us desire to be the best version of ourselves; we long to communicate in compelling and inspiring ways. This book answers that need. It is my hope that the process described here will help you enhance both your voice and confidence so you can ultimately achieve your career goals.

Cecilia Wessinger leads a 1 Million Cups meeting

# Chapter 1
# Powering Without Pressing

"Self-assured speakers command our attention with their conviction, not their arrogance. They speak to higher principles and for the greater good but do so in a genuinely humble manner. Projecting self-assuredness is not about positioning yourself as 'the expert,' meeting perfectionist standards, or allowing the ego to run wild. Arrogance, flawlessness and dogmatism are merely the illusions of self-assuredness."
Christine Jahnke[1]

## Why Voice is Important

Our relationship with our own voice is surprisingly complex. It is connected to the core of who we are. It is linked to our past, our emotions, our motivations, desires, and to our health. Our voice reveals our essence to the world. Whether we are confident, secure, happy, healthy, inspired or intimidated, our voice tells all. It is no secret that desire and sincerity alone are not enough to get you where you want to go. Even full knowledge of a subject or years of experience in your field may not be enough. The impact you make on others in the workplace is a combination of personal qualities that affect not only **what** you say but **how** you say it. No personal quality speaks louder than the voice. An individual's ability to use the voice in an expressive, open, relaxed, clear and articulate manner is a tool for success in virtually any modern arena. A skillfully used, dynamic, and expressive voice will serve your message and seize your audience, whether it is in a small conference room, a court room, a large lecture hall or TV interview.

We certainly live in a visual society: looks are very important. Research published in the *British Journal of Social and Clinical*

*Psychology*,[2] an often quoted study by Albert Mehrabian, stated that 55% of communication is visual, 38% is tone of voice and 7% is word choice. Is that really a true representation of the power of our voice as a communication tool? To better answer this question, I conducted an informal experiment of my own to see what impact voice has on professional success. I asked a group of women to stand in front of a panel of observers. Each panel member was given a form on which they were to rank each woman's leadership potential. The first ranking was taken on appearance alone, without voice: on a scale of 1-5, who looks like they will be an effective leader? Then each woman spoke from a brief script. The panel was asked to rank them again. Based on voice alone, some women went way up on the leadership potential scale, some went down. If the voice was pleasing or had gravitas, they were perceived by the panel to have more leadership potential even if initially they did not have a "leadership" look. If the voice was described as childish or abrasive, they went down on the leadership potential scale.

Make no mistake, voice matters. People make judgments about us as soon as we open our mouths, as soon as we utter a word. Right or wrong, we are found to be educated or not, professional or not, calm and confident or not, acceptable or not, hirable or not, believable or not. These assumptions are often formed solely on the quality of our voice and clarity of our speech. A reassuring thought here – it is much easier to change the way you sound than it is to change the way you look!

**Why women lose their voices**

Stand in the middle of an elementary school playground and hear children raising their voices in play. If you cover your eyes, you won't be able to tell the difference between the boys and the girls. They shout, command, rejoice, get angry, share, reject, lead and follow. Children sound the same.

Stand in the hall in a junior high school, and it is a different sound. Boys are louder, girls are softer; and it is not just the biology of boys' voices developing. New rules, both spoken and implied, are made evident to both girls and boys from teachers, parents, peers and the media, which define acceptable behavior and voice. Boys are encouraged to be independent, to speak up and to lead. Girls historically have been encouraged to "tone it down." To be popular, the supreme goal of most young women, you have to be less vocal, less loud and less bossy. While boys are typically praised for assertive behaviors both at play and in the classroom, girls are frequently admonished for the same behaviors.

For many girls the energy and confidence voiced in childhood go into hiding. To maintain harmony, we learn to keep up the illusion that we are perfect little ladies; we learn to contain the voice. In her book *In a Different Voice,* Carol Gilligan writes "…many women feared that others would condemn them or hurt them if they spoke, that others would not listen or understand, that speaking would only lead to further confusion, that it was better to appear "selfless," to give up their voices to keep the peace."[3] We learned these lessons early and for many of us the patterns of deferring, of speaking softly, of letting our actions speak for us, of compromising and of accepting less can stay with us for a lifetime.

Now skip ahead a couple of decades and we notice the behaviors which were rewarded by teachers, parents and peers don't serve us in the professional world. Employees who advance to the highest levels of leadership speak up, make decisions quickly, think and act independently, confidently tell their story to employees and motivate groups to unified action. Those of us who have played by the "perfect little girl" rules find ourselves at a distinct disadvantage.

Don't despair. There are some encouraging statistics reported by Katty Kay and Claire Shipman in their book *The Confidence Code*.[4] Women in the United States now earn more college and graduate degrees than men and run some of the greatest companies. There are seventeen female heads of state around the world. Women make up half the workforce and there is a high percentage of women in middle-management positions. In 80 percent of American families, women control the spending decisions. By 2018, many wives will out earn husbands.

Even as these facts give us cause for optimism, at the time of this writing, just 21 companies in the Fortune 500 are led by women. Women still undervalue their own worth, expecting less pay than men for a similar job. Underestimating their potential earnings, they are less likely to negotiate a salary increase. Women speak up less often, feeling they don't have anything to say, fearing they will not be taken seriously or appear foolish. Women who speak up are labeled as aggressive, pushy and self-promoting. In *How Remarkable Women Lead: The Break Through Model for Work,* authors Brash, Cranston and Lewis say, "these excuses mask deeper fears of being found out, being ridiculed. Fear drives many of us to set an unrealistically high bar that would stop anyone."[5] When a man sees a job description, he will apply if he meets 60 percent of the required skills and experience; the average woman will only apply if she meets 100 percent of the requirements.

When a girl or a young woman suppresses her voice for any of these reasons, her voice will go to one of two default settings. First it may go into hiding, staying soft, quiet, childlike and self-deprecating. I call this **"Denial."** We all know this gal - her voice is thin and soft, unsupported by breath, choked in the vocal tract. We notice that her shoulders are slightly rounded the head hangs forward. Her voice has caved in on itself.

The second default setting, and on the other extreme, is "**Bluff**." This is the woman who projects, "If I am going to succeed in a man's world then I will sound like a man!" Her voice is strident, aggressive or pressed, traits that are frequently called out in employee evaluations as "You come on too strong." We notice that her shoulders are drawn back, the chest is high and the chin is lifted.[6]

These examples – Denial and Bluff - are obviously two extremes. In my own life, I have exhibited both in different situations. The **authentic voice** rests in between Denial and Bluff, where we can find **"power without press**." The authentic voice lives in the **grounded, centered**, easy body. It is only from a place of ease that we can access our true power, the place from which our voice is strong, clear and compelling.

## *Voices from the field*

*When I fall into one of these traps, it will be "Bluff" every time. I spent years unlearning my physical rigidity. Certain vocal and physical tactics have helped me establish a genuine, confident presence without leaning into "Bluff." I can be grounded without having my feet glued to the floor. I give myself the freedom to move with purpose through a room at key points in a presentation. And as someone with a naturally louder voice, I have power without having to push for it; it was all about relaxing enough to let my breath do the work."*
    *Anna Fearheiley*

*I had witnessed women who just pushed their way in, like a bulldozer, with a chip on their shoulder; as if someone is trying to take advantage of them. With that kind of demeanor, what they are actually communicating is they don't belong there. I was determined to hold my own without ever being rude. I believed that if I was gracious, true to myself and held my own that I wouldn't ever have to be that way. I just kept asking questions and invited myself into meetings. If I felt any resistance I just asked, "How can I help you if I don't know?"*
    *Teri Aulph*

> 🎥 **#2 Denial/Bluff, Grounding and Centering, Power without Press**

## Exercise: Denial vs Bluff

For this exercise you will need a simple personal introduction statement which includes your name and your business or title. For example, "My name is Rena Cook and I am the founder of Vocal Authority."

1. Stand in your **familiar** way. Bring awareness into your body. Be aware of your head and neck, where your shoulders are, where your hips are, where your weight is distributed over your feet.
2. In your familiar stance introduce yourself using the introduction statement described above. Without judging, be aware of how that sounds and feels.
3. Now allow your shoulders to round forward, slump a little, your head comes forward, your pelvis settles back. This is the **Denial** stance, see Jade in the illustration below. As you stand in this way, certain feelings or thoughts may start to flow, like "I am not prepared. I am not ready. Everyone else is better than I am."

4.  In Denial, say your introduction statement. What does that sound and feel like?

5.  Still standing, draw your spine up long and tall, pull your shoulders back, stretch across your chest, lift your chin. This is the stance of **Bluff** (notice the changes in Jade's alignment as she goes to Bluff). Now say your introduction. How does that sound and feel?

6.  Now adjust your stance. Relax the shoulders down a bit, but not drooping forward. Feel the back of your neck long, feel soft front of neck, chin is parallel to the floor, your feet are hip width apart and your weight is evenly distributed. This is your **natural stance**. Say your introduction again. Is this different? What does the voice sound like? What do you think it conveys?

In this simple exercise we went from Familiar, to Denial, to Bluff, to Natural Stance. **Authentic voice -** a voice that is powerful without press - comes from this natural stance, balanced, upright, but not rigid or held**.**

## Grounding

Grounding is a term we use when we speak of our stability, our foundation which starts with our feet. The feet must always be in solid contact with the floor. A sense of **gravitas**, the quality that projects inner confidence, comfort and quiet power is built upon this foundation – an awareness that the feet are connected to the floor, drawing energy up from the earth.

## Exericse: Grounding

1. Stand in the natural way we experienced earlier – long back of neck and soft front of neck. Place your feet hip width apart, point your toes straight ahead and soften your knees. Imagine that the base of the big toe, the base of the little toe and the heel form a solid triangle of support. Keeping the knees released, stand firmly on that base and relish the sense of strength it gives you.
2. Rock forward on your toes, then back on your heels several times. Rock side to side across the bottom of your feet. Find that place where the weight is evenly balanced over both feet. Imagine the bones in the foot spreading out across the floor.
3. **Feel** as though you can draw energy and support from the earth. Imagine that energy is drawn up through the soles of the feet, the whole of the earth is supporting your body as it speaks and moves.
4. Speak your introductory phrase and enjoy feeling the sound coming up through your body from your grounded base.

## Centering

If grounding has to do with feeling the feet against the floor, centering has to do with the awareness that your power center is just below the navel. Place your hand on your lower stomach and image that all your thoughts, opinion, emotions and experiences are housed in your center, under your hand. When we are pressing, the energy goes high in the chest as the chin juts forward to prove a point. When we speak weakly or breathily, the energy dissipates before our words can leave our mouths. If we shift that focus to our center and believe that the center is leading us through space or guiding our thoughts and inspiration, it puts our power lower in the body where it is more effective and reliable.

**Exercise: Centering**

1.  Stand with feet hip-width apart, knees relaxed, shoulders down, long back of neck and soft front of neck. Feel the grounding of your feet, the energy coming up through the floor. Place a hand at or just below your navel. Focus on your center. Imagine the video of your mind that is playing in your head all the time is actually located in your center. It is like a camera lens, not at eye level, but at your center.
2.  Envision a hoped-for accomplishment: asking for a raise, expressing the perfect thought at a meeting, adeptly steering a conversation to your point of view. Turn on the video camera in your center and see it happening there. Not in your mind's eye, but in your belly.
3.  Now speak your introduction from this place of powerful awareness. Be aware of how little effort you need from the waist up if you are grounded and centered.

## Power without Press

Here is Robin demonstrating alignment for power without press.

Many successful speakers, leaders and politicians come to me with a common, often insidious problem. They find their power through pressing - through working too hard in the wrong parts of the body, as Jade is demonstrating in her previous illustration. When I see shoulders pressed back, chests coming forward and chins lifting I know what kind of sound I am going to hear – shouting, grating, abrasive, forced or husky.

This will never be ultimately effective because it is not authentic, not inviting, not convincing and will always be vocally fatiguing to the person speaking. Hillary Clinton is a perfect example. On the campaign trail, when she wanted to rally her crowds, her voice went into overdrive, shouting and pressing. Audiences tire of this type of delivery pretty quickly.

I teach, instead, to relocate the center of power to the lower abdomen. This is a way of thinking about how energy is produced and how it emanates from your body. If you release habitual tension in the body, ground and center, feel the breath deep in your torso, you will find an easier yet stronger source of power. When you want to "dial up" power or volume, focus on engagement in your center. The rest of the body, particularly the shoulders, head and neck, stay released.

To help you feel power without press in your own body try the following exercise:

1. Give each foot a good shake. Ground and center yourself as you did in the previous exercise.
2. Soften your knees and feel your neck lengthening.
3. Breath slowly and deeply
4. Say "ha" through a big, easy, open mouth.
5. With each new breath, say "ha" again, each time feel a little more engagement from the abdominals. Feel a little pulse in your belly on each sound. It is as if you are dialing up the energy, one notch at a time without tensing anywhere else in the body. Stop when you begin to feel the throat tensing up.
6. On a new breath, say a big open "hello." Feeling engagement in your center. Check your neck and shoulders to make sure they stay loose and free. Let the sound roll out a big open mouth. Try the word "tomorrow" in this same way. Then say "tomorrow and tomorrow and tomorrow," feeling the power from your abdominals, in your lower belly, while keeping the shoulders and neck free.

As we build on these beginning exercises you will become more and more acquainted with the "power without press" feeling. This is always where we start and where we return – it is our touchstone for all the work to follow.

**Reflective Journal:** Record what you experienced as you worked through the Denial/Bluff exercises. Did one feel more familiar to you? What did you hear or feel in your voice as you moved between these default stances? What did natural, authentic stance feel like by contrast? What are your thoughts about grounding? At what point did you feel the most change or shift? Where in the body are you most aware of change? What is happening with the breath? Have your feelings or emotions shifted at all? How did your voice change as your shifted your source of power to your center?

_____
_____
_____
_____
_____
_____
_____

Staying grounded and centered isn't easy. It takes practice and daily attention. On the days that I feel shaky and uncertain, I am comforted by the words of Leila Janah, founder and chief executive of Samasource, "You have to be willing to embrace the struggle. If you want anything great in life, you have to be willing to go through the dark and painful moments of building something. Nothing great has ever come out of the easy days...only through struggle is our character really tested."[7] And with practice, every day, we can stay present and grounded so we are better able to confront the challenges with clear, strong and authentic voices.

### Voices from the field

*One of our many challenges as women at work is the pressure (whether internal or external, real or imagined) to be simultaneously feminine, sexy, maternal, funny and a trustworthy, competent leader. Traits that are stereotypically "sexy" (soft voice, soft gestures, artful glances) are opposed to the recipe for confident, authentic communication. Some habits we may have accidentally picked up along the way must first be broken down to make room for new skills. If "power without press" feels inauthentic at first, give it a few weeks of practice. Soon you'll find yourself armed with an aligned posture and a stronger, healthier voice – suddenly, communicating with these tools becomes natural because it's your body's favorite state of being!*

*It is also helpful to note that an authentic, expressive voice is equally helpful in one-on-one or small group situations. Whether it's time to have a serious discussion about an employee's performance or to pitch a new project, the ability to communicate clearly and openly is invaluable.*

*Anna Fearheiley*

Rena reminds Alissa to release tension in her neck

# Chapter 2
# Releasing Habitual Tension

"Leaders take charge, but a woman with a dominant style can be viewed as too abrasive or pushy. The glass ceiling is cracked, but women still wage battle against sexism, low self-esteem and stage fright...the male voice still dominates the public square. As long as women remain a vocal minority in corporate boardrooms, on TV talk shows, and in the halls of Congress, we pay a price for being voiceless. The world needs well-spoken women to state opinions in every venue from PTA meetings to presidential debates."
Christine K. Jahnke[1]

"When the self-critic is present, you exhibit a stilted monotonous voice, a rigid body and eyes that are not seeing. In other words the person speaking or performing is not present – only the self-critic."
Meribeth Dayme[2]

A woman stands before a group of potential clients. It is her job to clarify an important point of the presentation. She knows her colleagues are depending on her. Thousands of dollars hang in the balance, as well as her reputation as a capable member of the team. Going through her mind is, "Oh god, why did I ever think I could do this? I am going to crash and burn. There is no way I can do this. They are going to fire me!" She feels a knot in the pit of her stomach, her shoulders draw closer to her ears, her breath is rapid and shallow, and her knees are locked (see Robin in the illustration above). When she opens her mouth to speak, the sound is barely audible, not like it sounded when she practiced. Her face flushes, her knees begin to quiver. Does any of this sound at all familiar?

Tension murders the voice. The inner critic, with her endless litany of negative mental messages, causes tension, which murders the voice. Tension anywhere in your body will shut down the voice, shut down the breath, shut down connection to your authentic spontaneous self and shut down your ability to be fully present. We have all fallen victim to this. In that moment it feels as if we are at the mercy of our body and these responses are beyond our control.

There is a cure for this mysterious ailment. Taming the demon of performance anxiety is possible. Tension in the body can be dispelled. You can shut off your inner critic. You can stop murdering your voice.

Let me pose a question. Does the body follow emotion or does emotion follow the body? Like the chicken-or-the-egg analogy, it is actually both. Emotions go where the body goes and the body goes where the emotions go. In my work with actors I have found that it is easier to control the body than it is to control the emotions so my daily practice, which includes my warm-up ritual, always begin with the body. Although I acknowledge tension is the inevitable byproduct of living in a modern world, it is the enemy of the authentic, expressive voice. Tension, anywhere in the body, stifles sound and muffles articulation. Learning how to release habitual tension is one of the first steps toward releasing a free, clear and dynamic voice. By releasing tension we find a state of "relaxed readiness."

The tension we normally carry in our bodies makes itself known through headaches, indigestion, muscle aches, joint pain, insomnia and free-floating anxiety. We are aware of the physical toll that stress and tension create, but most of us are not aware of the price we pay in our voices. The vocal folds (commonly called vocal chords) which actually produce the sound, are small, delicate membranes in the larynx, no bigger than the size of my thumb nails. The weight of any tension in the body eventually radiates and finds its way to the folds, causing them to work harder than they should. Hidden little tensions like toes gripping the floor, locked knees, a fixed pelvic girdle, a rigid spine, tense arms, fingers, shoulders, neck, jaw and tongue will eventually limit and stifle the voice.

Where does this tension come from? Just the fact that we, as human beings, walk upright in defiance of gravity, creates tension as we move through the day. Each vertebra is pulled toward the earth, causing the spine to compress. The weight of the head, twelve to fourteen pounds (about the size of a Thanksgiving turkey), is pulled forward. The shoulders move closer to the ear lobes, the back of the head sinks onto the top of the spine, the muscles that separate the ribs shorten, the chest falls toward the stomach, the knees lock and the ankles tighten. With this collapsing of space in the body comes a collapse of the voice as well. The voice has less space in which to live, less space to gather energy and vibrancy, less resonance, less volume and less brilliance. When space inside the body diminishes, the jaw, tongue, and vocal folds jump in to compensate, to help push the voice. This compensation only creates more tension, tightness and effort. The voice gets thin or strident and may feel scratchy and fatigued.

The simple activities of daily living – getting the kids off to school or arriving at work on time, performing well in a sales meeting, staying fit, pleasing bosses, spouses and colleagues - all cause the body and the voice to tighten. It is impossible to live in this world tension free. But it is possible to soften the body and the breath, to let the jaw hang loose, and to relax the tongue away from the hard palate. These simple, specific adjustments throughout a stress-filled day can make a huge difference. Releasing tension is a constant commitment and a daily challenge, and it is crucial to achieving a strong, clear voice.

The three quickest and easiest ways to release tension from the body and create space for the voice are to stretch, shake and breathe deeply. In the following exercises, we will do a little of each. As you work, focus each exhale on a gentle *fff* sound at your lips, and the inhale will take care of itself.

**Relaxation Exercise 1: Basic Preparation**

Before we start this sequence, create a simple introductory sentence or two for yourself, including your name and a statement of what you are most passionate about. Write it down here if you think you might not remember it easily.

_____

_____

_____

_____

Always start voice work with some variation of this basic exercise. It brings you to presence and shakes away tension so the voice is free to work.

1. Shake your hands.
2. Shake one foot, then the other.
3. Move your hips in a big circle.
4. Roll your shoulders.
5. Stretch up on your toes, arms reaching toward the sky.
6. Sigh out a huge sound of relief.

**#3 Internal Space Awareness**

**Relaxation Exercise 2: Internal Space Awareness**

In order for the voice to work in its most efficient and effective way, a feeling of space must be continually created in the body: space in the mouth, space in the neck, space up the spine, space between the ribs, space between the shoulders and earlobes, space across the shoulder girdle, space in the joints, space in the torso, space in the lungs and space in the abdomen. These are naturally occurring spaces in the body that collapse and get smaller as we pick up tension through the course of the day. Drawing awareness to inner space begins to free the voice as it relaxes the body. A quick note about volume and filling a large space: the more sense of inner space you carry with you, the more vocal power you will have to fill the larger space outside of you.

As you work through this exercise, remember to breathe; imagine that you can breathe into the spaces you are creating. Close your eyes so you can better envision the inside of the body.

1. Stand with feet hip-width apart, knees released, eyes closed.
2. Think of the top of the head floating up as if filled with helium, the face forward, the back of the neck long. Imagine that your neck is growing skyward with the chin parallel to the floor.
3. Feel the jaw relaxed and hanging loosely from the skull, with teeth slightly apart. Allow the tongue to rest on the floor of the mouth with the tip behind and gently touching the bottom teeth.
4. Feel the weight of the shoulders giving into gravity; be aware of the distance between your shoulders and earlobes.
5. Imagine a ball of energy moving out from the middle of the shoulders, widening and lengthening along the shoulders.
6. Imagine that your upper arm is moving away from your shoulders, the lower arm is moving from your elbow, your hands are moving away from your wrist.
7. See your rib cage as a large airy barrel surrounding your spine, imagine your lungs as two large balloons filled with air.
8. Imagine that your spine is growing in two directions as the head floats to the sky, the tailbone toward the earth. Be aware of the space between the vertebrae.
9. Be aware of the space between your hips and your torso. Imagine that the torso can move up and away from the hips.
10. Feel the space between your thighs and shins.
11. Imagine that the feet are spreading out against the floor.
12. Relish how tall and light you feel as you find space inside the body; breathe into all the new-found spaces.

13. With this new sense of inner space, let a breath drop in and speak: count 1-10, say your introductory statement. Be aware of changes in your sound.

Throughout this work, I will remind you of the importance of creating the image of space within the body. This sensation is one you want to maintain as you do this vocal work. Even under the pressure of speaking in public, if you start to feel that the voice is not working just right, simply think space and your voice will right itself.

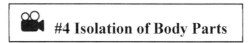

**#4 Isolation of Body Parts**

**Relaxation Exercise 3: Isolation of Body Parts**

1. Stand with your feet parallel, hip-width apart, with your weight evenly distributed over both feet.
2. Let a breath drop into your body and sigh out a robust sigh of relief; this brings your mind and breath into the body. Sigh out several more times on voice: a hearty "ahh." With each one, feel a deeper sense of relief.

The **neck**, where the vocal folds are housed, is a huge repository of tension. The goal here is to maximize your sense of space in the back of the head and neck. Each of the release exercises below should be repeated with gentle-to-moderate effort at least 10 times.

3. Let your chin drop to your chest and shake your head "no." Be aware of the gentle pull between the shoulders.
4. Let your right ear float near your right shoulder, then drop your chin forward onto the chest. Then let your left

ear float to the left shoulder. Go back and forth as if you are inscribing a "happy face" in the air with the top of your head. It is rather like a "suspend and fall" movement - the movement of the head suspends over one shoulder, and then falls as the chin returns heavily to the chest and rolls up to the other side.

5. Inscribe a circle in the air with the tip of your nose. Start with a small circle, then let it get larger. Reverse direction, going from large to small.

6. Head Float: Feel the top of the head floating up as if filled with helium; the sensation of "long back of neck, soft front of neck" is key and recurrent in the work. The face is forward, eyes on the horizon, as the back of neck lengthens toward the sky. Be aware of space between the head and shoulders and the space between the vertebrae in the neck.

The **shoulders** are a favorite spot for tension collection. As I go through the day, I find my shoulders getting closer and closer to my earlobes. As I sit at the computer, listen to an animated client or a frustrated colleague, or answer a sales question, I can feel that space getting smaller and smaller. Follow the steps below to enhance the space above and below the shoulders. Again, 10 repetitions is our magic number.

7. Circle the shoulders slowly, putting all your concentration into a controlled perfect circle. Feel the shoulder joint getting looser and wider as the size of your circle increases. Breathe deeply as though you can lubricate the shoulders with breath. Reverse the circle.

8. Bounce the shoulders gently, lifting them high to the earlobes and dropping them low and heavy.

9. Swing one arm in a large circle like a windmill, first in one direction, then the other. Swing the other arm in the same way.
10. Shake your hands by relaxing at the wrist and gently flapping up and down.

**Torso and Spine**: A physical therapist once told me that you are only as healthy as your spine. Keeping the spine supple and flexible with these simple daily exercises is part of the process for the good of the voice and the good of your general health. The following sequence should be done with an awareness of creating space between ribs, space between vertebra, and a general openness and expansion of the torso.

11. With arms loosely out from the body; gently twist your torso from side to side, increasing flexibility in the spine. This is a relaxed movement; do not throw your body from side to side, just let it go there.

12. As Erin is modeling in the illustration above, roll down the spine slowly, feeling the head giving into gravity, one

vertebra at a time, knees bent, head and arms remaining free all the way down. Shake out some sound, feeling it fall out the top of your head. Sigh out a deep sigh of relief. Roll up slowly from the base of the spine, again focusing on length and space. The neck and head are the last to come up. Be aware of the easy natural alignment of the spine, neck and head as you come to standing.

**Ribs:** The ribs, and the muscles between each rib, encase the lungs. If they are stretched and released the lungs can take a deeper, Easier breath.

13. To open the muscles between the ribs, reach your right arm over your head and stretch it toward the left, as Markeida is doing in the illustration below. Keep your knees relaxed as you imagine breathing into your exposed rib cage; hold the stretch for 5 breaths. Imagine that you are "presenting the rib cage," as if showing that exposed rib cage to the world. Then vigorously pat the rib cage. Let your arms relax at your side. Allow a deep breath to drop into your torso. Does the stretched side move more in response to the breath?

14. Repeat this stretch and pat on the other side. When both arms return to your side, be aware of the sense of lift and expansion in the ribs. You have created more space for the lungs to inflate with air.

**Lower body:** From the waist down, including hips, pelvic girdle, knees and ankles, we hold tension that we need to let go of.

15. To release the hips and pelvic girdle and create a sense of inner space, move your hips in a big, sloppy circle, like a hoola hoop, 10 times in one direction and 10 in the other. The knees stay released. Add an easy hum with your lips together, teeth apart. Open the sound to an "aah," letting the sound mirror the circle of the hips.

16. Put a gentle shake in your hips to give a final loosening to the whole area. Add as easy "ahh" as you move.

17. Lift your foot and circle at the ankle, first in one direction and then in the other. Think of a perfect circle in your ankle. Imagine that you can draw breath up through the

sole of your foot. Repeat 10 times in each direction with each ankle. Enjoy the space you have created between the foot and the rest of the leg. You can also add a hum as you circle the foot.

With the above exercises, you have loosened the body, released some of the tension that blocks the voice, gently warmed up your voice, and created inner space which will allow the voice to be more open, vibrant, resonant and clear.

18. Check back in with your voice by trying your introduction sentence again. Is there a difference?

**Negative Mental Messages**

From a body that is more relaxed and ready, let's address your inner critic. Negative mental messages stifle your self-confidence and increase insidious physical tensions. You know, those tapes of self-sabotage that we play over and over and over in our minds. Think of situations you have been in where you had a thought, an idea, or opinion but you bit your tongue, held your silence, or squelched your words. You probably don't have to go very far back to find an example. What did you say to yourself at the time? It may have been something like these:

No one will listen.
They will think I'm stupid.
It seems too obvious to even say.
I am new here.
Don't make waves.
It might be misinterpreted.
What if I am wrong?
I will sound foolish.

Add your own negative mental messages to this list. Write them down here.

_____

_____

_____

_____

These kinds of negative mental messages sabotage your voice, your confidence, and access to breath, creativity and spontaneity. In short they shut you down.

Now rewrite those negative mental messages here in positive terms. For example:

They will see I have something to offer.
I know I am correct.
I deserve to be here.
I know I am good.
I have prepared and I am ready.

_____

_____

_____

_____

Whatever your inner critic tells you, rephrase in the form of positive statements. Write them, repeat them, each time you warm up to face your day. The brain can be retrained! You can stop murdering your impulse to speak by changing the way you think about your verbal contributions.

One final but powerful exercise is to write your litany of negative mental messages on separate slips of paper. Then tear them up, wad them up and throw them away. The subconscious loves ritual. The act of writing and tearing will imprint on your brain that these thoughts no longer effect you.

When your body is released from habitual tension and your negative mental chatter is silenced, you will have stopped murdering the voice.

Try your introduction one last time.

**Reflective Journal:** What did you learn about your body and the release work? What was different in the way you felt physically, emotionally and mentally after the exercises? What questions came up for you as you worked? Which exercises worked best for you? Describe how you feel right now? Was there a part of the exercise where you sensed a feeling of inner space? What has changed in your voice? Where in the body does the voice feel most alive? How did it feel to tear up your negative mental messages?

_____

_____

_____

_____

_____

_____

_____

_____

_____

_____

## *Voices from the Field*

*Women are often hesitant to raise their hand and speak up. I learned if I waited, someone else would say exactly what I thought. It was my idea, it came from my brain and it is was worthy of being said. I knew if what I said was not correct, someone would give me feedback. And that was OK. If you receive criticism, you take on board what is helpful; you let go what is hurtful and not helpful. Someone's words to me can't change how I see myself!*

*Men have no problem speaking up, even when they don't know the question. Women let themselves be drowned out. I also feel women often can't say the hard stuff – there is a lot of talking around the issues while not addressing the real problem, whether it is race or a disparity issue. I coached domestic violence advocates, "you belong at the table with the police chief, as much as the district attorney. Don't relegate yourself to a committee. If you are on a task force, you need to be on the task force. You have equal influence and an equal perspective that needs to be shared."*
  *Felicia Correia*

*The women I have worked with, and I have found this to be true in myself, are less likely to press or be forced when they are confident. When we are settled in their minds that we are the one who should be talking or running for office, we have the expertise, the experience, we all tend to relax. We get to be more of our authentic selves, with less tension. I see less caving in, "denial as you call it," as well as less "bluffing," pushing to be like a man. With confidence comes relaxation, authenticity and presence.*
  *Aurora Gregory*

Alissa Mortimer inspires her students.

# Chapter 3
# Aligning for Presence and Ease

**"In addition to the external barriers erected by society, women are hindered by barriers that exist within ourselves. We hold back in ways both large and small, by lacking in self-confidence, by not raising our hands, and by pulling back when we should lean in. We internalize the negative messages we got throughout our lives-the message that says it is wrong to be outspoken, aggressive, more powerful than men...We lower our own expectations of what we can achieve."**
Sheryl Sandburg[1]

## Familiar vs Natural Alignment

Two women are in the same lobby waiting to be called in for a job interview. One is 5 feet 7 inches tall but her shoulders round down and her head and neck hang forward, her eyes are focused toward the floor. She sits with her arms folded and her legs crossed. The other is pacing the room, walking heavily on her heels, her shoulders are braced back, her elbows are sharp and her chin is elevated. I am sure you are already guessing how each will do in that interview. Neither of them realizes their bodies are communicating, even as they are unaware. Sometimes the messages we send out are not at all what we intend. People begin to make assumptions about us from the way we carry ourselves - the shape of the spine, whether it is long and straight or hunched and rounded, the position of the shoulders, or the lift of the chin. Our shoulders alone can say something about our level of confidence, social effectiveness, health and emotional maturity. Other people may even make assertions about personal discipline and intelligence based on how we carry ourselves – our alignment.

 Rena Cook

Our major body parts – head, neck, shoulders, rib cage, hips, knees and feet – are naturally organized to counter the effects of gravity, to ensure that we move comfortably and breathe easily. In voice terms, natural alignment creates a foundation for the voice. Lifting the body into its natural state creates space for the diaphragm to move, space for breath in the lungs, and space for resonance in the throat and mouth. Natural alignment allows us to look confident, feel calmer, and sound clear and authentic.

Throughout our lives, from our first steps onward, we have been forming habits of how we organize our bodies - how we stand, sit and move. We are responding to feedback we receive from parents and peers. We are fulfilling our social and psychological needs. We are defending ourselves against the natural stresses of existence. In short, we are trying to survive. Thus we develop our familiar alignment which may not serve us vocally or physically.

Many of us are not aware that our "familiar" alignment, what we have grown accustomed to through years of habitual use, may be sabotaging our vocal potential. The head may jut forward, the shoulders round forward or press back, the rib cage caves in or thrusts out, or the hips push to one side. The feet may not be making solid contact with the floor. You probably recognize yourself in one or more of these images and want to answer, "But, Rena, this is just how I always stand; that's how I move naturally." It may be how you are accustomed to standing or moving, but it may not be the most efficient way for your body to function. If you want maximum vocal effectiveness, you need to look at your alignment.
Let's look at the components of *natural alignment*:

- The top of the head floats and lifts toward the sky as if helium balloons are tied to the base of the skull.
- The head sits easily on top of the spine, the face is forward, eyes alert meeting the world.
- The chin is parallel to the floor.
- The shoulders are relaxed and down.
- The arms hang easily at the side.
- The pelvis is centered, neither tucked under nor pushed back.
- The knees are released (not locked).
- The feet are parallel, hip width apart with weight evenly distributed.

It is not only the voice that is linked to natural alignment, but physical and mental health as well. Notice the contrast in Erin when she goes back to her familiar alignment.

If your familiar stance is caved, slouched or rounded, your digestion can't work as efficiently; your back is compromised and will eventually lead to stiffness and pain, if it isn't already giving you problems. Also your physical state informs your emotional state. If we meet the world in a body that is not naturally aligned, we will likely feel a lack of self-confidence, with a dark, heavy or sad mood. We might even feel free-floating anxiety when there is no reason to feel uneasy or irritable. Poor alignment affects our ability to take a deep breath, so we may feel anxious due to lack of oxygen.

An adjustment in our alignment can lead to an adjustment in our sense of well-being. Notice the illustration of Erin below – she looks and feels more comfortable. When our lungs are given space to fully inflate, and breathe moves freely and deeply, it clears the anxiety chemicals from the body. And of course, with a healthy breath comes a healthy voice. With natural alignment comes ease – everything gets a little easier!

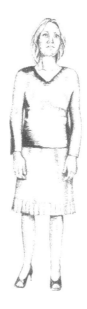

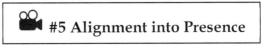

## #5 Alignment into Presence

## Exercise for Alignment

The following pages take you through natural alignment in detail. Some of these instructions are outlined in the previous chapter, but more details are added here to build depth of learning and change your internal focus. While working through these exercises, maintain a sense of ease as you go from your familiar alignment to your natural alignment.

## Feet

1.  Start with a grounded base, maintaining awareness of the feet in solid contact with the earth. Imagine that energy is drawn up through the soles of the feet; the whole of the earth is supporting the body as it speaks and moves.
2.  Place the feet parallel, hip-width apart.
3.  Shift your weight back and forth from one foot to the other several times. Rock forward and back from toes to heels. Find that place where the weight is evenly balanced over both feet. Imagine the bones in the feet spreading out across the floor.
4.  Imagine that the base of the big toe, the base of the little toe and the heel form a solid triangle of support. Keeping the knees released, stand firmly on that base and relish the sense of strength it gives you.

## Knees

1. Release your knees with a gentle bounce, find "oingo-boingo" in your ankles and knees. Be aware of space and ease in the joints.
2. For the sake of contrast, lock your knees and try to breathe. With your knees still locked say, "Good morning, I am so pleased to be here today." Now release the knees, take a breathe and repeat, "Good morning, I am so pleased to be here today." It should be clear that the locked knees make deep breathing more difficult, and that vocal ease, volume and clarity are negatively effected.
3. It is natural to lock the knees under the pressure of performance. It is part of the "fight or flight" mechanism that kicks in. A trained voice user knows to release, release, release at the start of the presentation, and at key points during.

Release of the knees should not be confused with bent knees. A speaker does not go through life with permanently bent knees. It is a simple release as opposed to a lock. Go back and forth between locked and released to become more aware of the difference.

## Pelvic Girdle and Tail Bone Awareness

The foundations of the torso are the pelvic girdle and tail bone. In the use of the free and released voice, they provide the floor of the inner space that we are attempting to create. The pelvic girdle contains a key to release and support, both crucial components in the development of the voice.

Common problems in this area have to do with the holding of muscles and habitual pelvic tilts, either too far forward or too far back. Each of these leads to breath problems and blockage of a fuller, richer and louder voice. Ideally, a speaker wants to sound as if the whole torso – all the way to the pelvic floor – is involved in creating the voice.

The following exercises will increase your sensory awareness of the pelvic girdle and the tailbone. They will also help you find length in the lower spine and feel where the most efficient and released position exists for you.

**Tailbone**

1. Imagine that your tailbone has an eye on it and can actually see behind you, in front of you, or at the floor. Move the pelvic girdle so that the eye of tailbone can see the wall in front of you. Push the pelvic girdle back so the eye of the tailbone can see the wall behind you. Then allow the tailbone to look at the floor right underneath you. Repeat this several times until you get a sense of where the tailbone is. Do this with ease.

2. Shake the tailbone to release any tension and say out loud an easy "ahh."

**Spine**

1. Imagine the base of the spine: think up the spine one vertebra at a time, easing and lifting all the way to the top of the head. It is as if your spine is growing from the top and the bottom. The tailbone is moving toward the earth, the head is moving toward the sky. The face is still forward, eyes open to meet the world.

2. Take a walk around the room, feeling the power in the spine. Your face is leading you forward, and the top of the head is leading you up. Be aware of the space between the vertebrae. Imagine you are taller. The feet are in firm contact with the floor; your arms are moving easily at your side.

3. Stop and re-align; think about the feet in solid contact with the floor, weight evenly distributed, knees released, length in the lower spine, the upper spine moving toward the sky, arms relaxed at your sides.

## Shoulders

1. Check to see that the shoulders are relaxed and down, the chest is wide, and the arms are hanging at your side.

2. Bounce the shoulders several times up and down. Feel the weight as they come up toward the ear lobes; drop the weight heavily as they give in to gravity. Vocalize an "aah" as you jostle the shoulders up and down.

3. Round the shoulders forward. Attempt to breathe and say the now familiar line, "Good morning, I am so pleased to be here today." This is what you sound like in *denial*.

4. Push the shoulders back. Again, attempt to breathe and say your line. This is what you voice sounds like in *bluff*. In either position breathing and making sound were probably not easy.

5. Bounce the shoulders up and down again and relax them in the down position. Feel the wideness of the chest. Breathe and say your line, "Good morning, I am so pleased to be here today." You should feel that breath is easier and sound is fuller.

**Head**

Think "long back of neck, soft front of neck, chin parallel to the floor." This is the position that creates the most space in the throat and back of mouth. Many of us are chin-leaders. We press, stress, and emphasize with our chin. As soon as the chin comes up, we have closed off the space in the throat and the back of the mouth. The jaw and tongue become tense. The voice gets brittle, shrill, tight, or under projected. From this position, the vocal folds have to do extra duty, which causes them to fatigue. As you explore the sensation of "long back of neck, soft front of neck," be aware that your jaw is released and the tongue is resting on the floor of the mouth.

1. Gently look right and left several times. Look down and up several times. Find a place of balance as the head rests on the top vertebra Drop.
2. Drop the chin to the chest and shake your head "no."
3. Slowly let it lift back to neutral.
4. Let your right ear drop gently toward your right shoulder and exhale on a "sh" sound. Let the head float back to neutral. Allow your left ear to drop gently toward the left shoulder, exhaling on a "sh" sound. Again, let the head float back to neutral. Do this slowly several times.

**Putting It All Together**

Natural alignment is an ideal: it is a starting point. Speakers often deviate from this as they get involved in the heat of the performance. But we start from and return to this place of natural alignment throughout a presentation or conversation, knowing this is the place of maximum inner space, support, ease and efficiency.

Let's review a quick check list for natural alignment.

1. Feet are in solid contact with the floor.
2. There is "oingo-boingo" in the ankles and the knees.
3. There is length in the lower spine as the tailbone lengthens toward the floor; the middle and upper spine extend upward as if floating toward the sky.
4. The shoulders are relaxed and down, arms hanging easily at your sides.
5. The head floats on top of the spine with long back of neck and soft front of neck.
6. The chin is parallel to the floor.
7. The jaw is relaxed, and the tongue is resting on the floor of the mouth.
8. The breath is flowing easily.
9. Take a walk around the room and enjoy the sensation of ease, energy and lightness.
10. Stop and re-align. Try your introduction or count easily 1-10.
11. Walk again briskly – not zombie-like, but alert and ready to do a job.
12. Stop and speak your introduction or count again.
13. For contrast's sake, try walking in your "familiar" alignment, your habitual walk, and say your introduction or count as you walk.
14. Now recover your "natural alignment," again creating space in the spine. Aware that breath is flowing in your body, walk briskly and speak. Go back and forth several times between familiar and natural alignment. Repeat your personal introductory statement or count. Be aware

of the differences in the effort, quality and volume of your sound.

## Forward Inclination and Natural Alignment

A simple and quick way to find natural alignment is through a forward inclination or spinal roll down introduced in Chapter 2.

1. Stand with your feet hip-width apart, weight evenly distributed, long spine, released neck. Breathe slowly and deeply throughout this exercise.
2. Let your chin drop to your chest. Slowly giving in to gravity, let the spine incline forward one vertebra at a time, until the head and neck are dangling free. The arms are released, the knees are bent and you are breathing deeply. Sigh out as if the sound could just fall from the mouth.
3. Start to rebuild the spine from your tail bone, stacking one vertebra on top of the other, like building blocks; the head is the last to come up. When the spine and shoulders are fully erect, lift the head, feeling long back of neck, soft front of neck and a released jaw. Breathe into your center.

How does this feel? What does this do for your sense of alignment? Does the spine feel longer? What is happening with the lower spine? The pelvic girdle? The jaw?

## Presence

Presence is the state of being fully aware of what is going on in the moment. We are fascinated by a person with presence; we want to be with them, listen to them, and trust them. Natural alignment communicates to others that you are present, you are grounded, centered and connected to deep central breathing. Your neck is long and easy. You are really seeing and hearing. The negative chatter in your mind is quiet. Your objective is clear. You are open and responsive to those around you. A person who is present projects an easy confidence. They are more aware of what is happening in the room than they are of themselves.

**Exercise: Components of Presence**

1. Feel your feet against the floor to make sure you are grounded.
2. Find the breath in your center.
3. Feel the back of your neck long, the front of your neck soft.
4. Say "My name is…and I am so glad to be here."
5. Say it again and mean it.

Don't rush into any professional speaking situation, meeting, presentation or discussion without first checking in to this feeling of ease and presence.

**Reflective Journal:** Record what you experienced as you worked through the alignment exercises. What are your thoughts about your familiar alignment vs. your natural alignment? At what point did you feel the most change or shift? Where in the body are you most aware of change? What is happening with the breath? Have your feelings or emotions shifted at all? How has it changed your voice? When you add attention to presence, what shifts?

_____

_____

_____

---
---
---
---
---
---
---
---
---
---
---

## *Voices from the Field*

*As a young professional woman, I was intimidated, I didn't speak up at meetings, I wasn't confident in that room. If I could go back and talk to my younger self, I'd say, "Rise to the occasion and be present! Be who you are, don't put on what you think is expected. Be your true authentic self. You have something to offer. You were hired for a reason. What are the skills you bring to the table? Your voice matters. Always be present." I used to disconnect because I didn't feel I belonged there. I didn't see my value. It took me until my 40s to figure that out. I finally found my voice and gained confidence. Use your strengths and passion – that's your voice! As I face big meetings, I prepare so I can bring my best, most present self through the door. Stay connected, listen actively and ask questions! If something is not clear – ask. Don't be afraid of stupid questions. Men ask stupid questions all the time and no one judges them.*

*Angela Byers*

Rena encourages Markeida to make space in her mouth for more vocal power.

# Chapter 4

# Breathing for Power

"To breathe fully is to live fully, to manifest the full range and power of inborn potential...it unleashes the energy of life providing pathways into the deepest recesses of our body."
Dennis Lewis[1]

"...As human beings with our own emotional, psychic, and physiological history we have developed habitual patterns of behaviour that feel safe, right, natural, and real. If we try to alter these patterns of behaviour, we may feel unsafe, wrong, unnatural, and false; particularly if we are in a situation of emotional stress, such as in training or rehearsal. Many of these behavioural patterns concern how we breathe – how we breathe for life, how we breathe to speak, how we breathe when we listen, how we breathe in different emotional states."
David Carey[2]

I joined the church choir at St. James Methodist Church in Tucson, Arizona, when I was in the third grade. I was just seven but I can still remember the first practice, where I sat, what I wore, what songs we sang. Though only two other children showed up that Sunday night, I sang boldly, undaunted. It never occurred to me to wonder if I had talent - it didn't matter. I didn't feel exposed being one of only three – it didn't matter. I just did what came naturally to me – I sang! That was the beginning a life-long love affair with all things voice.

I continued to sing in church choir, school chorus, took private voice lessons, studied acting, performed in musicals, and even made a record. All the while I was peripherally aware that breath was important. After all, every performance teacher I ever had told me so. But it wasn't until I was in London studying voice at the Central School in 1999, that I finally began to put it all together. David Carey, who provided the quote at the beginning of this chapter, was the course director. The underpinning of virtually every class he taught was breath – science, theory and practice. His clear and thorough knowledge of the relationship of breath and voice led me to an appreciation of the power of deep central breathing, which has now become the centerpiece of what I teach.

Breath is the single most important factor in the efficient use of the voice. If the breath is not working, nothing else will work. Breath is the cornerstone of the free and released voice, and no amount of intelligence, talent, preparation or sound systems can compensate for its absence. A responsive, flexible breath system translates directly to volume, quality, connection to authentic emotion and ease of delivery.

Breathing is both the easiest and hardest task for a speaker to master. When I first introduce the concept of breath for speech, no matter the age group, I get a response something like this, "But Rena, I already know how to breathe. If I weren't breathing I'd be dead." And I say, "Yes but there are two types of breath: breath that sustains life, which you do involuntarily, and breath for speech, which we will learn takes a little more thought, practice and attention."

**Breath is voice.** What we hear and identify as human speech sound is just disturbed air. We take in breath and, as we exhale, the breath stream passes over the vocal folds causing them to vibrate, disturbing the outgoing flow of air. So breath is the fuel which ignites the voice. The physical action of the movement of the breath is a natural and automatic response to the need to share the voice. It is a beautifully complex, integrated system that, through focus and daily practice, can become as easy as…well, breathing.

**Breath is the master key to our soul.** The deep central breath connects us to who we are, to the core of the human being that lives inside us, to our most authentic selves. Breath connects me to my intelligence, my creativity and my spontaneous response mechanism. I learned this through years of training actors. An actor can learn her lines and movements and execute them perfectly; but if breath is not deep and central in the body the audience will not be transfixed. The miracle of authentic communication cannot happen without it.

## How Breath Works

In order to help us understand how the breath works, let's imagine that the voice is like a trumpet. In order for the trumpet to sound you have to blow air into the mouth piece. Breath is the power source. If you want the trumpet to be louder you blow more air. It is the same with the human voice; if you want a louder, fuller sound, you need more air.

Indulge the voice geek in me here as we discuss the finer points of the deep central breath. As mentioned above there are two kinds of breath: passive breath for sustaining life, and active breath for speech. Breath to sustain life – both the inhale and exhale – happens unconsciously with minimal effort; the body instinctively does its job of keeping us alive. Breath for speech differs in that both the inhale and the exhale are conscious and take a certain amount of energy and muscular engagement. It takes a great deal of energy and breath to speak lengthy ideas, communicate weighty emotions, or fill a huge auditorium with sound.

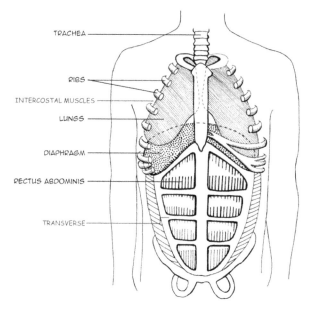

THE TORSO

Key anatomical players of the breath system are:

1.  The **torso** extends from the shoulders to the pelvic girdle, to the ribs on either side, and to the breast bone in front and the spine in back. It houses the ribs, lungs, stomach and intestines.
2.  The **diaphragm** is a large dome-shaped muscle that bisects the torso, positioned under the lungs and on top of the stomach.
3.  The **intercostal muscles** link the ribs and allow them to move up and out so the lungs can fully inflate with air.
4.  The muscles of the **abdominal wall,** specifically the **transverse** abdominal, are the muscles of breath support.
5.  The **lungs** inflate with air on the inhale and deflate on the exhale.

6. The **vocal folds**, located behind the Adam's Apple, the sound source, two flaps of tissue with a layer of muscle at the core that vibrate or oscillate when air blows past, creating tiny puffs of air, thus producing sound.

When breathing for speech, the brain sends a signal that it would like to say something; it has a thought that needs to be communicated with the voice. The body then prepares to inhale in readiness for speech. A release of the **abdominal wall** follows, the **diaphragm** contracts and drops down and the **ribs** swing out and up. This action of the diaphragm and the ribs creates a negative pressure in the lungs. Air rushes into the lungs to equalize this pressure.

When the lungs have sufficient air, the process reverses and the exhale begins. It is on the exhale portion of the breathing cycle that sound occurs. The diaphragm relaxes and begins a passive journey back up to its resting place. The ribs move down and in. The muscles of the abdomen, primarily the **transverse**, engage to manage the exhale in terms of duration and the amount of air that leaves the lungs. This muscular action of the transverse is what we refer to as "breath support." When a choral conductor says, "support your sound," or your speech coach asks you to "use support," what they mean is to engage the lower abdominals – the transverse – so you have adequate breath to support the voice for the length of the thought, phrase or sentence.

The exhaled air flow travels up through the **windpipe** where it meets the closed vocal folds. The air pressure builds up, causing the vocal folds to blow open and snap closed hundreds of times per second, releasing tiny puffs of air, thus producing sound. Imagine that the words are carried out on a stream of breath. Breath and sound are one. When the exhale stops, the sound stops.

## How Breath Goes Wrong

When I was a young performer I noticed that when I auditioned, my voice would become thin and lose power. I also found myself having to take breaths in places I had not before. I now know that the culprit was **high, shallow breathing**. When we are nervous or experiencing stage fright, chemical changes take place in the body. One of the first and strongest responses is the inability to take a deep breath. Under pressure, we instinctively resort to shallow breathing, which is not good for the voice and heightens performance anxiety. If your shoulders move up noticeably when you breathe in, you are filling only the top lobes of your lungs. That will not give you the breath capacity for a strong voice or the stamina to complete a complex thought without gasping for breath mid-sentence.

The majority of oxygen exchange happens deep in the bottom of the lungs. When we engage in high, shallow breathing, the oxygen never gets deep enough to nourish our brain, wake up our body, enliven our thoughts, trigger our creativity or calm our nerves.

Another way that breath for speech can go wrong is **weak abdominal release** on the inhale. When the abdomen releases, the diaphragm has more room to contract down, creating a larger space in the chest for more air to enter the lungs. Many voice users initially do what I call reverse breathing: they suck the stomach in on the inhale and push it out on the exhale. This leads to shallow breathing and a reduction in the ability to support the sound. Through the exercises that follow, we will learn how an easy abdominal release on the inhale is our touchstone. Remember, as the breath comes in, the abdomen releases and goes out. On the exhale, the abdomen, guided by the transverse abdominal muscle, moves toward the spine.

Another way that breath for speech can go wrong is **lack of breath support** on the exhale, leading to insufficient air moving past the vocal folds. When the vocal folds do not receive a strong, steady stream of air for speech, they must work too hard, causing the voice to be pressed, strident, thin and small, or lacking in range of emotion, volume and quality. Lack of breath support can result in vocal fatigue at the least and permanent damage to the vocal folds at the worst.

We have already talked about **generalized tension in the body** and how it can sabotage the deep central breath. Locked knees, a rigid pelvic girdle, a tight stomach, a restricted rib cage, and tension in the shoulders, jaw or tongue all inhibit the system. This kind of tension is insidious because we are often unaware of its presence; it is so common that it feels normal to us. Locking the knees is an unconscious response to standing for a long period of time; couple that with any level of performance anxiety, and those knees want to lock up tight. The shoulders tend to creep up to our ears because of the tension we pick up throughout the day. Tension anywhere in the body creeps into other parts, setting off a chain reaction in the body. Localized or generalized body tension prevents the abdominal muscles from fully releasing, keeping the diaphragm higher, creating less space for lungs, which are then forced to take in smaller amounts of air, causing the vocal folds to do double duty. You get the picture.

The following exercises for the breath fall into six categories: 1. Connecting to the natural breath that sustains life, 2. Releasing the abdominal wall which precedes the inhale, 3. Sensing the moment of readiness, 4. Engaging the transverse, which manages and supports the breath on the exhale, 5. Building breath capacity and sustainability, 6. Accessing support and 7. Connecting breath to words. For some of these exercises you will need 5-6 sentences from your 60-second elevator pitch or vision statement. If you don't have one yet, write out something that will give you a script to use.

## Connecting to the Natural Breath

For the following two exercises, you will need a drinking straw and a balloon.

## Exercise: Balanced Breath Through a Straw

The purpose of the first exercise is to experience an easy, balanced breath while bringing attention to the natural movement of the abdominal area which is your center. You are going to inhale and exhale fully through a drinking straw.

1. Gently hold the straw in the middle and put it between your lips.
2. Exhale through the straw on a slow four count. Then inhale through the straw on a slow four count.
3. As you inhale and exhale slowly through the straw, put a hand on your belly so you are aware of what is happening in your center. As you exhale, your center will move toward the spine. As you inhale the center will release easily out.
4. Repeat this for several minutes.

If you have panic issues associated with breathing, the exercise *will not* trigger an attack. If you start to get dizzy, reduce the effort.

## Exercise: Blow up the Balloon

The purpose of this exercise is to give you a strong sense of what the center does when you are breathing for speech.

1. Stretch the balloon so it will blow up easier. Blow up the balloon at your own pace, taking in a new breath when you need to. Put a hand on your belly again and be aware of what is happening in your center.
2. Be aware of movement of the transverse and of how automatic it is. The abdomen expands as you inhale - the deeper the breath, the larger the expansion. On the exhale, the transverse engages and moves toward the spine.

Under normal circumstances, we seldom need the amount of muscular engagement in the abdominals that you needed to blow up the balloon. Think of that as effort level 10. For normal speaking, one to one or in a small group, you may only use effort level 3-4. A truly responsive breathing system is easy and natural, happening without conscious thought on your part. That's why we train – to teach the body what it must do on its own – so that in the heat of presenting, we are free to concentrate on the real issues, like what we want to share and if that message is getting across.

---

📹 **#6 Breathing for Power: Abdominal Release, Sensing the Moment of Readiness, Recoil Breath, Trampoline Breath, Building Capacity and Breath Management**

---

## Feeling Abdominal Release

Release of the abdominal wall is a challenging concept for a culture that worships the flat stomach. Many of us expend a lot of energy and effort to keep the stomach held in at all times. However, the speaker must learn to cast aside that ideal and embrace a belly that is relaxed, even (dare I say it) "poochie," on the inhale. On the inhale the stomach area expands; on the exhale the stomach moves toward the spine.

## Exercise: Abdominal Release

1. Stand easily in natural alignment and be aware of how you are breathing. Stay with this for at least 10 breaths. Don't try to change it, just be aware of your own breath rhythm. Where are you most aware of the breath entering and leaving the body?
2. Place a hand just below your navel, and feel the abdomen release into your hand on each inhale.
3. Blow all the air out of your lungs on a "fff" or "sh" and wait until your body needs a breath. When your body signals that a breath is needed, release the abdominal wall and feel a breath drop in. Repeat this sequence 5 times. Blow out all the air, wait for the need to breathe, and then allow a breath to drop in. You should feel the abdomen release and expand on each new inhale.
4. Now let the natural breath rhythm just happen – the breath comes in, the breath goes out. Be aware of the

56

pause that occurs after each cycle – breath comes in, breath goes out, pause. Repeat several times.

5. Continue exploring the breath cycle – the breath comes in, breath goes out, pause. Enjoy the pause, luxuriate in it, and wait gently for the need to start the cycle again. Notice that the quality of the pause determines the quality of the next inhale. Keep your knees soft, the back of the neck long and the jaw hanging loosely.

Breathing in this way should feel natural and easy.

## Sensing the Moment of Readiness

This exercise is one you will want to revisit over and over to make it a part of your daily warm-up. You can do this standing in natural alignment or sitting easily in a chair.

## Exercise: Moment of Readiness

1. Find the natural rhythm of your breath: the breath comes in, the breath goes out. Notice the pause. When that rhythm is deeply established, turn your focus to the moment when the inhale becomes the exhale. Feel it deep in your torso. It may feel like a momentary suspension, an easy change of direction. Stay with this awareness for several breaths.

2. Once you have established the awareness of the moment when the inhale turns to the exhale, mark that point with the word "now." Keep the knees soft, the back of neck long, and the jaw released as you sound "now" each time the inhale becomes the exhale. Repeat at least 10 times.

3. Holding the awareness of the moment when the inhale becomes the exhale, lengthen the "now." Repeat several times, still focusing on the inhale becoming the exhale.

4. Keep this focus and, with a big space in the mouth, let the sound lengthen to the full extent of the breath, saying "Now, even now, even now, even now." Repeat several times until you can feel that perfect moment of readiness: the point in the breath cycle when the inhale becomes the exhale and the body is ready for sound. Memorize what this feels like. Enjoy how easy it is to create full, rich open sound with so little effort.

5. With the knees still soft, the neck still easy and long, and the jaw still released, change to the phrase to "Tomorrow and tomorrow and tomorrow." Feel it fly from your body; let the sound reach all the way across the room and touch the wall. Keep focusing on the moment when the inhale becomes the exhale. Repeat at least 10 times.

6. Change the sound to your introduction, "My name is… and I am/do…" Repeat several times, still sensing the moment of readiness when the inhale becomes the exhale, then speak.

7. Try four or five sentences from your 60-second elevator pitch or your personal mission statement. Breathe at thought changes, while maintaining the focus on the moment when the inhale becomes the exhale.

**Engaging the Transverse Muscle with the recoil breath**

1. Say "sh-shhh" with enough power to expel all your air. Feel the recoil of the transverse muscle as it quickly and naturally releases to let the next breath come in. Repeat 4 times.

2. Change the sound to "v-vvv" and repeat 4 times. Do the same with "z-zzz."

**Trampoline Breath**

1. Find your natural alignment, grounded and centered. Place a hand gently on your transverse muscle.
2. Say "ha ha ha" quickly and lightly as if a little man is using your diaphragm as a trampoline. Repeat the "ha" until you need a breath, then let a breath fall in and repeat 3 times. Put a hand on your center so you can feel the activation of the transverse muscle. Effort level should be between 3 and 4. Keep your jaw released and the tongue resting on the floor of the mouth.
3. Say "hee hee hee" as if that same little man is jumping on the trampoline of your transverse. Repeat the sound until you need a breath, then let the breath fall in. Repeat 3 times.
4. Say "ho ho ho" in the same manner as above.

At the end of this simple three-exercise sequence, you should feel that your transverse muscle have been engaged and enlivened. These exercises should be part of your standard daily vocal warm-up.

**Building Breath Capacity and Sustainability**

The following exercises will help you in several ways. First, you gain a kinesthetic or physical understanding of the amount of breath needed for the size of the thought. A short thought requires a smaller breath; a longer thought requires a bigger breath. You will develop the capacity to sustain an even flow of breath to match the length of the thought. In addition, you will increase the flexibility of the breath as you easily move from short to medium to long thoughts.

## Capacity

1. Imagine that you are blowing out a single candle. Now imagine that you are blowing out 10 candles. Then, blow out 100 candles.
2. Imagine you are holding a feather in your hand. Blow the feather off your hand. Keep the feather in the air with a stream of breath. Blow a hand full of feathers across the room. Blow away all the feathers from a huge pillow that has burst open.
3. Put your finger to your lips and gently "shush" a talkative movie patron seated a row in front of you. He does not get the message, so "shush" him louder. Then, "shush" him as if you would push him out the door with the force of your breath.

Notice, in each case, that you took the amount of breath necessary to fulfill the requirements of each escalating situation. As the circumstances became more urgent and the need larger, the amount of air taken in and the amount of force behind the released air also became larger.

Note: If you begin to feel a little light-headed or dizzy while doing these exercises, take a break until it passes.

## Breath Management

This exercise helps your body learn the lessons of breath management from a short thought to a long thought. This time, the thoughts are going to take the form of numbers: 1- 10.

Find easy natural alignment. Knees are released, back of neck is long and jaw is released. Say "one." Breathe. Say "one by two." Breathe. Say "one by two by three." Breathe. Continue on in this way to "ten." Be aware of what is happening in your center as you progress. Be aware of the ease of each new breath. The body knows how much breath it needs for the length of the thought coming next. This exercise should become a standard part of your vocal warm-up.

## Building Breath Capacity

1. Stand in natural alignment. Blow out all your air quickly on a "shhhh," and when you need a breath, let one come in. Begin an exhale on "zz." Continue as long as you can comfortably sustain the sound. Don't go so long that you start to tighten or sputter. Renew the breath, and sustain the "zz" four to six times.
2. You can also do this exercise on "ss." Try it both ways and see which sound is easier.

By doing this kind of exercise every day you can double your capacity in a couple of weeks. This should also become a standard part of your vocal warm-up.

## Breathing the Space

Doing breathe work at home or in your coach's studio feels easy and safe. We think we have mastered it. Then when we move into the larger space, we suddenly go back to shallow breathing and pressing to achieve the volume required to fill the space. Use your introductory sentence and a sentence or two from your 60-second elevator pitch or personal mission statement for the exercise below.

When you transition from small space to large space try this exercise:

## Exercise: Breathing the Space

1. Raise the palm of your hand to about 16 inches from your face. Breathe that distance and speak several sentences of your introduction or elevator pitch to your hand.
2. Extend your arm fully and breathe to the tips of your fingers. Speak the sentences to the end of your hand.
3. Now look at the center of the room. Breathe that space, feel a little more space in your mouth, and speak to those seats, resisting the temptation to press.
4. Now focus on the wall furthest from you. Breathe that distance, and speak your introduction. Resist the temptation to press from the vocal folds. Think more space in the mouth, keep the thoughts clear on your lips, and release your knees. If you fill the body with breath and open your mouth you will be able to fill the space with sound without pressing or shouting![3]

I have a few tips about dealing with dizziness or lightheadedness, which happens frequently when doing breathe work. Keeping the knees released will help. Reducing the effort can help. Opening the eyes and focusing on the palm of your hand can steady you. Taking a break from the exercise for a few moments may also be helpful.

## Accessing Support by Pressing Against a Wall

Support was defined earlier in this chapter as the abdominal muscles, primarily the transverse, engaging to manage the flow of the exhale as we speak. If you want more vocal power or volume, you dial up the energy or engagement of the abdominals. If you have a long sentence or a large emotional thought you engage your abdominals for an extra boost. When we are first made aware of the importance of support, and we have never done it, we may need a quick and easy kinesthetic nudge as what that is and how it feels.

## Pressing the Wall

1. Stand facing a wall. Place both hands on the wall, slightly below shoulder height. Lunge forward with your dominate foot to give you a stronger base. Press your hands against the wall at a moderate energy level, enough so you feel the abdominals engage, but not so much that you feel tension in your throat. Breathe in then speak, counting 1-10 or your introduction. Feel the engagement around your middle powering your sound. Keep your throat open so it feels like a megaphone for the power in your center. When we want more power or volume our natural tendency is to press from the throat. Imagine that your power control is in your center and your abs are doing all the work. As you press into the wall and explore support, keep the back of your neck long and the front of your neck soft. Don't let tension radiate to your vocal folds.
2. Now step away from the wall, speak again. Try to maintain the sense of engagement you felt in your center as you pressed against the wall.

## Connecting Breath to Words

1. Following the breath exercises, it is vital to connect the sentences of your speech to breath. You do this by reading through your speech with a singular focus – to breathe at each punctuation. Use any speech that inspires you.
2. Read it out loud, breathing at each major punctuation. Take your time and find the moment of readiness at each new breath. Your body memorizes where the breaths go just as your brain memorizes the words.

**Reflective Journal:** Reflect on the straw, the balloon, abdominal release and sensing the moment of readiness. What did you learn about the breath that you did not know before? What did you learn about capacity, sustainability, and breath management? Which exercises gave you the most easy and natural sense of the breath as it moved in and out of your body? What is the moment of readiness like for you? Describe in your own words how it feels. How does this awareness affect the voice? What questions came up? What did the speech feel like as you breathed at each punctuation?

---
---
---
---
---
---
---
---
---
---

## *Voices from the Field*

*I have coached a lot of women around confidence for public speaking and job interviews. First you have to believe you are worthy. You may just have to fake it a few times. Eventually you start to believe it. And breath is so important – in a meeting if you get anxious your breath gets shallow and you notice that your shoulders are up under your ears. When that happens to me, I feel it and I reset my breath. Women don't ask for what they want. They are afraid to ask for a new position or a raise. I tell them not to back down. Don't allow someone else to determine your value. If you want to be part of the game and have a seat at the table as an influencer, your voice needs to change to match the strength of the message. How you say something is as important as the message…and you have to breathe.*

*Teri Aulph*

Markeida Johnson inspires her congregation.

# Chapter 5
# Building Authentic Confidence

"In the most basic terms, what we need to do is start acting and risking and failing, and stop mumbling and apologizing and prevaricating. It isn't that women don't have the ability to succeed; it's that we don't seem to believe we <u>can</u> succeed, and that stops us from even trying."
Katty Kay and Claire Shipman[1]

"My anxiety manifests itself in different ways. Sometimes it's just in my head and feels overwhelming, as if I've agreed to do too much. Other times, when I'm really nervous, my leg shakes, and then I look like a real crack-head at some luncheon where I've been asked to speak about being a powerful woman…. Whether I am stressed about working out, or speaking publicly, or showing up when I feel too tired, I always tell myself, 'Push through. This is only temporary.' Time goes by, even if you have something you're dreading, that feeling will not last forever…And if you push past the fear, you've accomplished something and you're a stud again."
Chelsea Handler[2]

"Personal power…implies having an innate sense of yourself that does not depend on what you think other people think, the ability and confidence to find out or ask what you need to know to do your job…the ability to listen to comments and criticism…to take care of your own needs…to maintain your energy and sense of self-worth."
Meribeth Dayme[3]

My journey toward authentic confidence has been a roller coaster – now I have it, now I don't. Sometimes it felt like a momentary loss, other times it was days, weeks, even months. When I made the move from teaching high school drama to higher education, I experienced a crisis of confidence. I feared I didn't belong there. "Who am I fooling, I am just a high school teacher, masquerading as a professor." I was apologetic and uncertain in all I said and did in my classes. Of course the students picked up on this and took me to task, pointing out missteps and misspeaks with glee. My end-of-term evaluations reflected this, one even saying, "She should go back to teaching high school." Ouch.

I remember crying, calling friends for moral support and thinking I had taken on more than I was capable of. Over winter break, I did some serious soul searching. In the midst of this confidence crisis, I was observing a fellow professor, Jack Wright, who was the epitome of the model college professor – beloved, talented, nurturing but challenging; students scrambled to take his classes and audition for the shows he directed. While weeping and wailing, I started to ask, "What would happen if I acted as if I were Jack Wright?" Not pretend to walk and talk like him, but carry the ease and confidence that he always carried with him. In the spring term I tried out my new resolve – "act as if." And the students bought it! Almost immediately, their attitudes and behaviors toward me changed. I began to feel better, my confidence genuinely began to escalate and I finished that semester with much stronger evaluations. I behaved in a confident manner and my emotions followed. My body led and belief followed.

I know I am not alone in this tale. Many of you have experienced times when your confidence failed you or you denied yourself an adventure, an opportunity, or a relationship because of lack of confidence. I am sure many of you make less money than you are worth because you lack the confidence to go after the raise or the promotion.

I interrupt the voice sequence here because the confidence work must follow the breath work. New and greater confidence cannot happen unless the breath is deep. The information and work that follows will take you through a process that develops both the mind and the body to build more authentic confidence.

What is confidence? What does it look like, and how can we get more of it? Consider these thoughts in terms of what you have witnessed or experienced yourself.

Confidence has energy, joy and focus.
Confidence has no anxiety or fear.
Confidence lives in an open, relaxed body, where deep breath is flowing.
Confidence has a strong, clear voice without apparent effort.
Confidence is a synchronization of talent and skill.
Confidence takes risks, knowing that failure, though possible, does not kill.

**Let's do some writing in your Reflective Journal on this topic.**

What would confidence look like in you? If you had all the confidence in the world and knew you could not fail, what would you do? What in your life drains you of confidence? What are your habitual negative mental messages that shut you down?

_____
_____
_____
_____
_____
_____
_____

As a gender, women are still having a crisis of confidence. There is on-going pay disparity between men and women; but it is not just a wage gap, it is a confidence gap. For example, if a man and a woman are both looking at the same job description, a man will apply if he has only 60% of the job's required skills, but a woman will not apply unless she has 100% of the skills. Women negotiate for a pay raise less often; and when they do, they expect less. In a room of mostly men, a woman will be reluctant to speak. A man in a room full of women will speak as much as he always does.[4] My dear friend and frequent co-presenter, Diana Morgan, gave one of our groups this advice:

"I think it's important to understand the dynamics of sexism and oppression so that we can better understand what we are up against and have compassion for ourselves. I don't think we are served, however, by focusing for very long on the injustices towards women. In fact when I do so I become ill. I think the most powerful thing we can do is to use this information as a springboard into action, taking risks, speaking up and growing our confidence. Women have come a very long way and while there's still a way to go, our fore-mothers and fore-sisters worked for the freedoms that we now enjoy. As a woman I feel a lot of freedom and I am thankful for that. I intend to keep growing and risking, finding my voice and building my confidence."

Confidence is part biology. We come into this world with a predisposition toward or away from confident behaviors and feelings. There are three neurotransmitters that play a huge role in confidence: serotonin, oxytocin and dopamine. Serotonin has the ability to inhibit anxiety. It helps us make calm, rational decisions because we feel less stress. Serotonin calms the amygdala, the fear center in our brains. Oxytocin, known as the cuddle hormone, generates warmth and positive attitudes. It creates the desire to hug, have sex, be generous with friends, share, and be faithful. It's heavily tied to optimism and paves the way for people to act and take risks. Due to our genes, some of us have more oxytocin than others. Dopamine, known as the adventure chemical, inspires doing and exploring, curiosity and risk-taking. The absence of it creates passivity, boredom and depression. Based on how our genes express, some of us have more dopamine than others. When it comes to confidence, dopamine gets us moving, serotonin induces calm thoughts and oxytocin generates warm and positive attitudes towards others.[5] So our biology can give us a kick start or a setback right out of the starting gate.

Confidence is also part nurture, which is how we were brought up. Did your parents foster or squelch confidence? Even if nature dealt you a weak confidence hand, nurture can shore you up. If your parents and teachers were dedicated to building confidence by providing activities in which you could succeed, gave support and encouragement for you to take risks and helped you learn resilience when you fell short, you could thrive with a high degree of confidence intact. Our upbringing has a huge effect on our adult level of confidence.

Most important for our work, confidence is also part choice. If both nature and nurture let you down, you will have some challenges in the confidence department. You can, however, overcome these and build confidence. The brain is plastic, it is malleable and always changing. You can teach your brain to think different thoughts, to have different beliefs. New neurotransmitters in the brain can be formed through specific exercises and daily practice. You can practice being confident and if you do the exercises on a regular basis, your brain and your emotions will start to believe a new truth. You can override genetics and childhood environment. So, life choices matter. Fairly simple brain training or methods of thinking can carve new pathways in our adult brains, pathways that encourage resilience and confident thinking and can become part of your hard wiring. Confidence is a choice we can all make!

Backing up to Chapter 2, a choice you can make right now is controlling negative mental messages that can drain your confidence. Even if you did this activity before, do again with more focus and clarity. Write down your familiar negative messages. Then rewrite them as positive statements. Your subconscious will hear this and begin to believe it. New neuropathways will form and confidence will grow. But like anything worth doing, it does take time and work. There is not a switch that can be flipped or a button that can be pushed.

## Reflective Journal

Write down the negative mental thoughts that drain your confidence.

_____

_____

_____

_____

_____

_____

_____

Now write the positive re-statement of each sentence above.

_____

_____

_____

_____

_____

_____

_____

In Chapter 4 we learned the importance of breath for voice, but breath is also key to confidence building and taming performance anxiety. Below are two breathing exercises that calm, quiet and focus the mind and body.

**Exercise: Slower, Deeper Quieter, Calmer**

Sit comfortably in a chair with both feet flat on the floor and close your eyes. Begin to focus on the breath by thinking "slower, deeper, quieter, calmer." Feel your breath slow down, feel your belly moving with the breath. You should hear no noise as you inhale or exhale. Feel, with each breath, you get calmer and more confident. Repeat for at least 10 breaths.

**Exercise: 4-7-8 Breath**[6]

Sitting comfortably with eyes closed as you did before, inhale for 4 counts, gently hold the breath for 7 counts and breathe out for 8 counts. Repeat at least 5 times.

These two breath exercises help to ground and center not only your breath but your emotions and your body energy which are foundations of authentic confidence.

**Exercise: Visualize Success**

Before you start this exercise, have a copy of a brief introduction, mission statement or 60-second pitch ready to use at its completion.

1. Still sitting comfortably, with your eyes closed, breathing slowly and deeply, tune into the sounds around you. What do you hear close to you? Imagine there is a circle of sound near you. What do you hear all around you in that circle? Extend your ear a little father, imagine that the circle is larger, father away from you. What else can you hear in this outer circle?

2. Tune in again to your breath. Begin the slower, deeper, quieter, calmer pattern. Imagine yourself in a speaking situation, interview, or negotiation, any situation that might have caused you anxiety or a loss of confidence. See this in detail. What are the surroundings? Who is present? What are you wearing? What are you saying? See yourself shinning, confidently using your voice, asking for what you want. Imagine everyone listening to you attentively.

3. Continue to breathe slowly and deeply. As you bring the visualization to a close, open your eyes, stand, ground yourself and speak. Feel the ease, confidence and energy in your center. Be aware of any shift in how you sound. This ease can be yours, each time you need it by going back to this visualization exercise. You can do it the morning of an event, or a few minutes before as you warm up your body and voice in preparation to bring your best self fully to the task at hand!

## Reflective Journal:

Nothing builds confidence better than action! Make a list of small things you can do that perhaps you have not had the confidence to do. Maybe it is picking up the phone to actually make that cold call, volunteering for more responsibility, or talking to a colleague about a challenging issue. Push yourself out of your comfort zone.

---
---
---
---
---
---
---

Once written, give yourself a challenge to do, one per week, or one per day. Take one small risk. Small successes work together to build confidence.

**Gratitude:** Create a list of the positive traits you possess. Celebrate your strengths as part of your daily meditation. Example: I am generous with my time. I have a sense of humor.

---
---
---
---
---

**Write out accomplishments you are proud of.** Read them out loud or use in meditation. If you are working with a partner, say these out loud to her. Then listen attentively to her accomplishments.

_____

_____

_____

_____

_____

**Meditate daily:** Meditation does work! It alters the chemical makeup of your system, producing less fear and more calm in the brain and consequently throughout the body. I take ten minutes at the end of my daily workout to focus on breath, using the exercises introduced here and in Chapter 4. Recite the positive affirmations which grew out of the "eliminating negative mental messages" exercise or from "celebrating your strengths." Repeat those to yourself as you breathe slower, deeper, quieter and calmer. If you are not in the habit of meditating, if may feel awkward at first. But a few minutes every day will make lasting change in your authentic confidence and general anxiety level.

**Grounding and centering**, which we discussed in Chapter 1, is also a component of confidence. A person who is not grounded and centered will never be perceived as having confidence. Alignment, discussed in Chapter 2, is a component of confidence. Breath, discussed in Chapter 4, is a component of confidence. All these systems intertwine and synchronize to create the best version of you possible and firmly secure your authentic confidence!

## Owning the Room

Owning the room starts in the hall, outside the door. Take a moment to feel your feet against the floor, soften knees, connect to breath deep inside you center, relax shoulders, smile and walk through the door. Owning the room is taking authentic confidence and opening it to include all who are in it. Executive presence expert Silvia Ann Hewlett adds that to own a room "you must first read it. Sensing the mood, absorbing the cultural cues, and adjusting your language content and presentation style accordingly are vital."[7] When you are able to own the room, you no longer focus on yourself; you are focused on the needs of the group.

A young woman was in the audience as I shared the voice and confidence work outlined in this book. Following the two-hour presentation she emailed me this success story: "My lungs were filled with gratitude as I gradually released the love during a brief appearance for a news feature. Because of what I learned at your presentation, I humbly welcomed the opportunity to speak in front of a camera. I practiced as much as I could remember from your session for the brief televised interview. I remembered to align my body, keeping my chin parallel to the ground, mindfully grounding my feet and did many rounds of the 4-7-8 breathing exercise to relieve my nerves!" She attached the news clip and she was just lovely.

Confidence is built through taking risks and succeeding. The young woman in the story above took a risk. With some new knowledge and a technique, she prepared and succeeded. Look for small challenges in your professional realm, lay the groundwork for success through preparation and raise your hand. Then celebrate your success. Don't let your habitual negative mental messages tell you, "It was just a fluke." Counter that with, "I was successful because I am good. I prepared and I succeeded. I can do it again."

## Reflective Journal: Sharing Your Vision

I am sure each of you has a vision for your future, a vision for your children's future or a vision for our nation. As we progress with the voice work, I'd like you to have a paragraph that is meaningful to you, that comes from your heart and you care deeply about. Write your vision below. I would rather you work from a script so you focus on *how* you say it and not on *what* you say.

_____

_____

_____

_____

_____

_____

_____

_____

_____

_____

As you practice your vision statement out loud, your confidence will grow. Be sure that you remember to:

1. Ground the feet, soften the knees, lengthen the back of the neck, and find the moment when the inhale becomes the exhale.
2. Speak it out loud and breathe at each punctuation.
3. As you speak it again, imaging that you have been granted extra confidence from an unseen power.
4. Speak it as if your life depended on it.
5. Speak it to an imaginary audience – your children, boss, or spouse – and they are going to believe in every word you say.

6. Then just say it. Don't think too hard about doing it right – just release it!

**Reflective Journal:** How has our attitude toward confidence changed? What is our plan for building confidence as you move forward? How much time are you going to dedicate? How will you know when you have achieved success?

_____
_____
_____
_____
_____
_____
_____

## *Voices from the field*

*I encourage young women to make sure your voice is at the table. Take the risk to express your opinion. Have your facts ready. Women have an advantage in that we often have higher emotional intelligence and we can use that to read a situation. We can speak to the person where they are and that makes for better communication. We all need to trust the gifts we have to read the room, negotiate and to help find resolutions.*
    *Kathy Taylor*

*I advise young women to challenge themselves. Try different things as often as possible and learn from those experiences. You must take risks and break out of your comfort zone to grow confidence professionally and personally.*
    *Cheena Pazzo*

*I was 40 when I was "yanked up" the corporate ladder. Within just three years of leaving Norman, OK, I was on a company jet three days a week. I never got on the jet that I didn't think, "They are going to figure out who I am and send me home." Every day I was on the edge of my comfort zone. It was scary on a regular basis. We must have resilience and tenacity. We have to challenge the status quo and assumptions. It may seem insurmountable but, in reality, we can do this, one board room at a time, one relationship at a time. We have to be prepared to keep up.*
    *Teri Aulph*

Rena shows Melanie how to project to the back row.

# Chapter 6
# Empowering Resonance

"The research is overwhelming. Not only does the sound of your voice matter twice as much as what you're talking about…but voice in lower frequency range will encourage others to see you as successful, sociable, and smart…a high-pitched voice, particularly for women, is a career-stunting attribute…shrill voices have the hint of hysteria that drives men into a panic…A woman with a high-pitched tone will be perceived as not only unleaderlike but out of control."
Silvia Ann Hewlett[1]

## My mouth is my megaphone.

We all know the voice Ms. Hewlett is taking about in the quote above – fingernails on a chalk board. The word "frequency" is more meaningful to me than "high pitched." The perceived pitch of a woman's voice has more to do with resonance than it does with the highness or lowness of your actual pitch. Resonance is maximized very simply by making space in the mouth. Your mouth is your megaphone. If you want more sound, open your mouth. If you want more vocal warmth, open your mouth. If you want to sound more leader-like, open your mouth. If you want to sound more accessible, open your mouth. It is that easy and it is challenging, particularly if your lifelong habit is to speak through a very small space.

To understand this concept, let's dig a little deeper into what resonance actually is. How do you know the difference between the sound of a violin, a cello, or a stand-up bass? What is it about the quality of the sound that identifies each instrument? How would you describe a trumpet's sound in contrast to a tuba? A trumpet is bright; a tuba is full and rich. Just as each musical instrument has a distinctive quality, each human voice has attributes that are unique and have an emotional effect on the listener.

Can you describe the difference between the voice of James Earl Jones and Fran Drescher of *The Nanny* fame? Soothing, dark, comforting for Jones as opposed to piercing and brittle for Fran. Or Gwyneth Paltrow and Roseanne Barr? Gwyneth's sound is warm, mellow or smoky, while Roseanne might be bright, nasal and abrasive. Which voice would you rather listen to? Most listeners respond positively to Jones and Paltrow, negatively to Drescher and Barr, even as we admire and laugh at their comic abilities.

We use the word **quality** to describe that distinctive, individual sound. A component of vocal quality is **resonance,** the process by which sound created at the vocal folds is amplified, enriched, and filtered in the resonating chambers of the body. In a very general way, I think of resonance as disturbed air (breath that has been set in motion by the vocal folds) bouncing around the hollows of the body gaining energy, amplifying some qualities and dampening others. These body hollows make up the **vocal tract**: the throat, the mouth, and the nasal cavity. Resonance in the vocal track is your body's natural amplifier. Think of these as the bell of your trumpet.

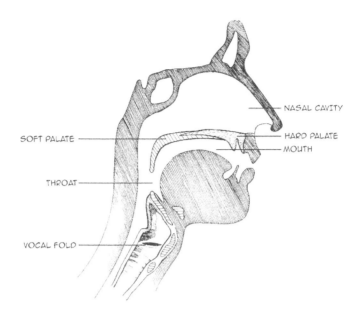

NASAL CAVITY

SOFT PALATE

HARD PALATE

MOUTH

THROAT

VOCAL FOLD

The trombone has a larger, lower tone than a trumpet. Why? It has a bigger resonating tube. Likewise, the tuba will always have a bigger, deeper sound than the trombone because it has the biggest resonating tube. Our resonating tube has an advantage over brass instruments in that ours is flexible, it can be made longer, shorter, wider or thinner. If you lengthen your neck, extend your lips forward, smile broadly or close your mouth slightly, you have changed the shape of your resonating tube which changes the quality of your sound. I maintain that it is more about a woman's resonance, easy space in the resonating tube, than her pitch that makes a voice pleasing or not.

Taking the brass instrument metaphor a step further, what happens when you put a mute in the end of the trumpet? The sound is muffled. The human voice has natural, built-in mutes - the jaw, tongue, and soft palate - that can likewise muffle our sound, dampening resonance and making quality less compelling. If our mutes are filled with tension, they can suffocate the quality of our sound. If they are open and relaxed our voice will be warmer and more inspiring. Our task then, as speakers, is to make sure our resonators are open and free of tension. In this chapter, we are going to focus on three parts of the vocal tract: the **jaw**, the **tongue** and the **soft palate**, all of which can house hidden tensions which dampen and restrict resonance.

The **jaw**, in voice terms, is a large hinge that serves as a gate-keeper to aid in the suppression and control of strong emotions. The masseter, the muscle that opens and closes the jaw, is one of the strongest in the body. The effort expended in keeping the jaw rigid results in tension, which backs up into the throat and stifles the resonance. To maximize space in the throat, we need to relax the jaw. It is not about creating a big space at the front of the mouth; it is about releasing the jaw, creating space and length between the back molars. The jaw should naturally drop straight down as it opens and releases to gravity. Keep in mind that tendons link the jaw to the throat and finally to the larynx itself. Tension in the jaw radiates to tension in the vocal folds. If the jaw remains held or tight, the vocal folds will also tighten and constrict, causing them to work harder, leading to loss of power, ease, and clarity.

The **tongue** is a huge muscle, often with a mind of its own. We are aware of the front or tip of the tongue because it is what we can see, but the real culprit is the back or root of the tongue. It can carry tension that we are not even aware of, pulling back and down into the throat, muting our sound and dampening clarity and warmth.

The **soft palate**, which lies at the back edge of the hard palate (roof of the mouth), has limited mobility but what it has can be maximized. The soft palate also has few nerve endings, so it is harder to feel and challenging to control. A flat palate can dampen sound and give the voice a nasal quality by allowing air to escape down the nasal cavity. We want a lifted palate, which creates a big space in the back of the mouth and maximizes oral resonance for speaking in large spaces.

I frequently speak of resonance in terms of vibration; when resonance is activated, we feel vibrations in the throat, jaw, face, chest, and sometimes even the top of the head. As speakers we want to maximize vibrations and to open our body up to them.

The following set of exercises promotes the opening of the vocal tract and the releasing of vibrations, thus maximizing the resonance of the voice.

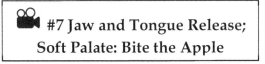

**#7 Jaw and Tongue Release;**
**Soft Palate: Bite the Apple**

**Exercise: Jaw Release**

1. Clench the jaw. With your fingers find the place where you feel the knot or tightness and rub that spot. Now release the clench and let the jaw hang as you continue to massage at the jaw hinge.
2. To further release the jaw, use the heel of hand to massage the jaw hinge in downward motions. The focus is on releasing the jaw to gravity, not forcing it open. With each pass of the hand, the jaw releases a bit more. Repeat five times at a slow rate of speed, and remember to breathe.

3. Take hold of the chin with both your hands - thumbs underneath, forefingers on top - and open and close the jaw with your hands. Imagine that the jaw is passive, that the hands are doing the work. Remember to keep breathing and maintaining a sense of length in the back of neck.

4. Easily chew in forward circles as if eating very chewy taffy. Do not move the jaw side to side. Think of easy circles that go down and up. Repeat ten times.

5. You might want to sanitize your hands before doing this exercise. Cross your hands at the wrist. Put your thumbs inside your mouth and press them against the jaw hinge, that hard spot between your upper and lower molars. Press straight back into that spot. Sustain a medium amount of pressure for at least five seconds. When you release, open and close the jaw to see if an easier space has opened up. This is acupressure for the jaw. Repeat this one more time.

6. Relish the feeling of a loose jaw, released and hanging. Lips can be open or gently closed as long as you maintain a feeling of space.

**Exercise: Tongue Release**

1. While the jaw is hanging loosely, having given into gravity, shift your focus to the tongue. Be aware that the tongue is resting on the floor of the mouth, with the tip gently touching the bottom teeth.

2. Allow the tongue to fall out of the mouth past the lips. Feel it lengthen gently toward the floor. Then stretch it gently toward the ceiling. With tongue still hanging out, send it toward your right ear, then to your left. Allow the tongue to gently clean the lips as if you have just taken a

bite from a big juicy peach and you don't want to miss a drop. Clean the inside of your mouth with your tongue.

**Exercise: Tongue-Speak**

This is a silly exercise, but it has a profound and immediate effect. Try it just once and I know you will be a convert. I use this as part of my everyday vocal warm up and again right before I present (clearly not in front of an audience – that's what bathroom stalls are for).

1. Let the tongue hang out of your mouth, and count out loud from one to ten, keeping the back of the neck long. Relax the tongue back into the mouth, letting it rest on the floor where it normally does. Count out loud again with a sense of a released jaw and tongue.
2. Say a few lines of your vision statement in tongue-speak, allowing the tongue to hang loosely out of the mouth. Then speak the same text with the tongue easily back in the mouth.

Be aware of the ease that is created when the tongue and jaw take their rightful places as relaxed articulators and not as tension spots forcing you to artificially create a louder sound.

**Exercise: Soft Palate**

1. Yawn widely with the tongue gently against the bottom teeth. Enjoy the yawn – stretch with the arms as if you have just awakened from a restful night's sleep. Be aware of a huge space opening at the back of the throat. Do this several times to remind the throat that being open and released allows for optimal resonance.

2. Sound the consonant "ng." To make this sound the tongue and soft palate come together. Feel the point of contact. Release the "ng" into an "ah" and feel the tongue and palate move away from each other. Repeat the following sequence slowly: ng-gee, ng-gay, ng-gah, ng-go, ng-goo. Feel the tongue and palate coming together on the "ng" and moving apart when you open to the vowel sound.

3. Imagine that you have a big, red, juicy apple in your hand. Lift it to your mouth and prepare to sink your teeth into it as if to take a large delicious bite. Feel the lift of the soft palate. Repeat and just before your teeth are ready to sink in say, "Hello," or perhaps, "Tomorrow and tomorrow and tomorrow." Repeat the bite of the apple each time you refresh the breath, creating a large, easy and open space. At the moment of readiness say, "Why fly so high," or "Four score and seven years ago," or "Ask not what your country can do for you, ask what you can do for your country." You can also use lines from your introduction or vision statement. On each new breath, lift the imaginary apple as if to bite. Speak through that easy, open space.

Through these two exercises you are building an awareness of the lifted soft palate. You are also teaching the soft palate, through muscle memory, the raised position for confident speech that carries forth effortlessly.

**Exercise: Humming to Increase Vibrations**

1. Humming is one of the easiest ways to release vibrations and increase resonance. Start a comfortably low hum with a big space in the back of the mouth. Hum until you

feel the need for a breath, then breathe and start the hum again. Tap gently on the chest to loosen the vibrations. Feel that you can fill your upper chest with vibrations. Keep the back of the neck long and the space in the back of the mouth wide.

2. Raise the pitch a little and continue to hum with a long back of neck and a big space between your back molars. Move the hum around on your face or chew so that the facial muscles are moving the hum around. Explore various pitches in the lower to middle part of the voice as you continue to hum.

3. Blow through the lips on a hum (think of horse lips). Let the pitch vary in small loops as you blow, widening the loops of pitch as you continue to hum. This gathers and increases the strength of vibrations and begins to loosen the pitch range.

4. To bring vibrations forward say: key, key, key, key, key. Speak this on a middle pitch, keeping the back of your neck long. Aim these vibrations on the back of the upper teeth.

5. Intoning is singing on one note comfortably in the middle of your range. In this exercise you are going to intone the phrase "My mother makes marmalade." Find a pitch in the middle of your range and sing the phrase on the same note, really enjoying the "m" sounds. Then *speak* it in the same pitch where you felt the intoning. Even if you think you don't sing, I encourage you to play with this – you have a beautiful voice!

6. Next, intone these phrases: "My mom makes more money than most men." "Many more moms making much more money." After you intone, speak the sentence in the same place you felt the energy of intoning.

7.  Finally, take a bit of your vision statement or 60-second elevator pitch and intone it. Breathe at the end of each thought until you have intoned the entire speech. Feel the vibrations forward in your mouth. Then say your speech with attention to the spot where you felt the most vibrations while intoning.

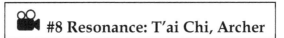 **#8 Resonance: T'ai Chi, Archer**

**Exercise: T'ai Chi Sequence**

This exercise is based on a T'ai Chi sequence. It contains three basic movements accompanied by a sound progression. The goal is to connect vibrations to breath, waking up the voice easily and fully. This warm-up can be done toward the beginning of each session or at the end to bring all parts of the range in line.

1.  Stand in natural alignment with the hands easily in front of the thighs. Throughout the exercise keep shoulders down, neck long and knees soft.
2.  On the inhale, bring hands to shoulder height. On the exhale, push the hands back down as you make sound according to the sound sequence below.
3.  Again, on the inhale, bring hands to shoulder height again. On the exhale, extend arms straight out and then down as you sound.
4.  Next, on the inhale, bring hands all the way up and over the head. On the exhale, open arms out and down as you sound.
5.  The sound sequence starts with humming. All three movements – up and down, up and out, and up and over

– are done on a hum. The next sequence opens to an "ah." Then, change to "oo," followed by "eee." Finally, advance to any vowel, any pitch.

6. A fun variation is "Ninja T'ai Chi" which is any vowel, any pitch, and any movement. While sounding, you can move any way you want, using arms in extravagant circles, arches and loops. On each inhale, the hands come back to their original starting position.

**Exercise: The Archer**

This exercise warms up vibrations and encourages the whole body to open to resonance. It can be done as a part of larger warm-up. As this exercise also focuses the mind and calms performance anxiety, "The Archer" is an ideal single warm-up, if time for a full warm-up is not available. Erin demonstrates in the illustration below.

1. Widen your base so that feet are further apart, approximately 24 inches. Bend the knees a little, keeping the back straight and the neck long. Cup the left hand easily at the waist; the right arm is across the body with the hand flexed, palm out.
2. Exhaling on a hum, the right arm moves to the right across the body, until it is straight to the side. On the inhale, the right hand cups at the waist, and the left arm crosses the body.
3. Exhaling on a hum, the left arm moves across the body, until it is straight to the side. This movement sequence repeats, sounding the hum four or five times. The sound opens to an "ah," then "oo," then "ee," and finally any vowel, any pitch, repeating the physical sequence five times on each sound, (Thanks to David Carey for T'ai Chi and the Archer. He and his wife Rebecca Clark Carey chronicle their excellent work in *Vocal Arts Workbook*.)

## Kazoo for Forward Resonance

Forward resonance carries the voice out into space, making it easier to project to the back of most rooms. Many of us let our resonance fall backward, down into the throat. The purpose of this exercise is to feel forward resonance and practice it in a way that will help us carry the sound in a professional speaking situation. Deep, dark, chesty, male voices often fall so far back that they don't carry well. Some women's voices can sound nasally, a quality that is unpleasant to our ears. Another female habit that is growing in popularity is **vocal fry**, which is falling off the voice toward the end of sentences, letting the pitch drop to the bottom of the voice. Though it is heard on television sit-coms and in popular movies, it is a voice habit that sends many young women to the speech therapist when they start losing their voices.

**Exercise: Kazoo for Forward Resonance**

You will need an inexpensive kazoo. (I buy them in bulk from the local party supply store.)

1. Put the big end of the kazoo in your mouth and hum. You will feel vibrations around the mouth. Hum a tune just for fun; your school fight song is always a good choice. Now with the kazoo in your mouth, speak/hum a portion of your introduction, vision statement or 60-second elevator speech into the kazoo. Take the kazoo away, and speak the speech in the same place you felt the vibrations from the kazoo.
2. Do the whole speech, one sentence at a time, first with the kazoo and then without, speaking in the same place you felt the energy from the kazoo.

I once had a very talented student who had a terrible case of vocal fry, a habit that she had tried to break for several years. I had her put the kazoo on a string around her neck for an entire semester. Whenever she spoke in vocal fry, either socially or on the stage, I said, "Kazoo it!" She would say the sentence into the kazoo and *voila*, she was back on voice. If you have any kind of resonance issue, either too far back, in the throat, in the nose, or vocal fry, make the kazoo a part of your personal warm-up every day. It is a quick reminder to your body where healthy, clear, forward resonance should live. (Thanks to Kate DeVore for the use of kazoo as a forward resonance bio-feedback tool.)

**Exercise: Resonating Energy Centers**

This final resonance exercise is for those of you who want to make meditation a part of your daily practice and build the voice as well. It is an excellent warm-up for full body resonance and also for deepening the breath and extending the pitch range. It also has a calming and focusing effect.

The purpose of this exercise is to center the breath, encourage vocal vibrations, and open the body's receptivity to vocal resonance. This exercise can be done daily or several times a week. It generally takes ten minutes to engage with it fully.

1. Sit in an easily erect position, eyes closed, with a long back of neck, jaw released, and focus on your breath.
2. Focus on your tail bone and intone the vowel "eh" on a comfortably low pitch, imagining that you can send vibrations to that area. Repeat each sound to the end of the breath at least five times.
3. Focus your attention on the space just below the navel; the sound is "oh" (as in the word "go"), and the pitch is slightly higher. As you sound, imagine that the "oh" sends vibrations into and spinning out of the abdominal area. Strengthen the vibrations, and feel that space come to life from the energy of the sound vibrations. Repeat each sound to the end of the breath at least five times.
4. Next, the focus of your attention moves to between the navel and the sternum. The sound is "ow" (as in the word "out"), and pitch again moves naturally up a tone. Feel vibrations of sound move to and spin out of this area. Repeat each sound to the end of the breath at least five times.

5. Now focus on your chest; the sound is "ah." Feel vibrations move through the chest, lungs, and heart. Feel that area come alive with your sound vibrations. Repeat each sound to the end of the breath at least five times.

6. Shift the focus to the throat and mouth area; the sound is "oo" (as in goose). Feel the area come alive with vibrations as the sound spins through it. Adjust pitch up to maximize vibrations in the throat and mouth. Repeat each sound to the end of the breath at least five times.

7. Move the focus to the forehead; the sound is a hum. Adjust your pitch up so you feel vibrations in the forehead. Imagine that the vibrations are streaming out of the forehead. Repeat each sound to the end of the breath at least five times.

8. Now focus on the final energy center at the top of the head; the sound "ee" (as in eat) helps to move vibrations into that area. Let the pitch move up as well. Feel the sound vibrations spin out the top of head – imagine a long stream reaching all the way to the sky. Repeat each sound to the end of the breath at least five times.

9. Now let your voice glide easily up and down from the tailbone through the top of the head and back, using any of the above sounds. Just let the voice play. Be extravagant as you let the sound motor throughout your pitch range.

10. Slowly find your way to standing and to natural alignment. Try a few sentences of your introduction, vision statement or 60-second pitch to see if your body is more receptive to the vibrations of the voice, the pitch freer, the sound more released, the breath more deeply rooted in your body. (Thanks to Joy Gardner-Gordon for inspiring this exercise sequence.)

**Reflective Journal:** Take a few moments to reflect on resonance: what you have learned, where you have questions or confusions, what you have discovered about resonance and your voice. Think about jaw, tongue, soft palate, humming, and kazoo. What you have learned about space in the mouth? Which of the above exercises were most useful? Which were not so much? What did you learn about your own voice through this chapter? What do you plan to take on as part of your personal voice practice?

_____

_____

_____

_____

_____

_____

_____

_____

_____

_____

_____

### Voices from the Field

*I am repeatedly struck by how women (including myself) undercut themselves through their way of speaking. Upon reflection, trying to identify a woman whose speaking style I look up to is, in many ways, as frustrating as trying to identify female role models. A woman I frequently communicate with has adopted a strange style of droning on and on and on, laying out the question very carefully, but also implicitly sending the message that our time is not valuable. It drives me crazy. Another woman comes to mind who has an almost incomprehensible speaking style, full of "ums" and "ehs" and breathy, almost airheaded circumlocutions that is also incredibly frustrating/counter-productive and actually sort of passive-aggressive. In the absence of a role model, I am finding my own path to presence and clarity through a daily Buddhist practice that has allowed me to hear and notice my true self through chanting. I continue to try to apply this insight into my speaking voice, but remain both frustrated and amused by how difficult that continues to seem to be.*
        Ellen McClure

Melanie Fry energizes the crowd.

# Chapter 7
# Expanding Pitch Range

"Phrasing, inflection and pitch are what distinguish you as person worth listening to…As in music, it is important to deliver your words conscious of your narrative arc, lifting and dropping your cadence to emphasize key passages or points, paying attention to how you end a phrase…so your listeners sense closure and they consequently hang on to the last word and retain it before making room for the next thought. The uplift that younger speakers impose on the ends of their sentences…undermines the whole message by denying this closure.

Silvia Ann Hewlett[1]

"Banish Upspeak…the raising the tone of your voice at the end of a sentence in a way that suggests you are asking a question, not making a declaration…It is a psychological safety net; it discourages interruptions and encourages reassurance…it detracts from the validly of the your argument…Say it like you mean it.

Katty Kay and Claire Shipman[2]

The pitch of a woman's voice is perhaps her most talked about vocal attribute. We hear feedback such as, "Her voice is shrill, high, thin, or small; her voice grates, or she sounds like a little girl." Expanding pitch range is the goal of all good speakers and is relatively easy to do, given regular practice. Pitch is so important in the vocal development process that I have included is a whole chapter devoted to its understanding and integration.

We may understand the concept of pitch better in musical terms as in a note can be high or low. Although the speaking voice does not sustain pitch as in sung music, pitch is always present. **Pitch range** is the distance from the highest note to the lowest note that an individual voice can use – it is a range of pitches that a speaker has at her disposal. Most of us use only a few notes of pitch variety in our professional speech, and even less in our everyday speech. The developed voice can have up to eight or ten notes of usable pitch range. This is not to say we should use all ten within every utterance, but more dynamic highs and lows in pitch range makes us more compelling to listen to.

Pitch is the result of tension, or amount of stretch, in the vocal folds themselves. The more stretched the folds, the higher the sound; the more relaxed the folds, the lower the sound. Think of the strings on a guitar: the fatter, looser strings create lower notes, while the thinner, tighter strings generate higher notes.

We only have to think of the monotone teacher whose lecture drones on with no pitch variety to know that one-note communication puts us to sleep. The speaker who uses her full voice and pitch range to express her enthusiasm and knowledge of her subject engages and holds us. Think for a moment about your favorite speakers. What is it about their voices that keeps you interested, which draws you into their message? I'll bet part of their success has to do with an expressive voice that makes use of a wider pitch range.

In our contemporary relaxed culture, it is cool to vocally sit on the bottom of the range, to speak in our lowest notes. Young women want to be taken seriously or sound sexy so they use their lowest notes, what we now call vocal fry (mentioned in the previous chaper). There are, by contrast, some young women who keep their little girl voices long after they have physically grown beyond that. Perhaps for psychological reasons, they are hanging on to past behaviors and relationship patterns that feel comfortable. Continuously speaking in either extremes of the pitch range is not as effective for the professional female speaking voice. It limits expressive options, limits the ability to be heard and understood in larger spaces. It can also lead to vocal health issues where loss of voice can become a real possibility. Joanna Cazden, a speech pathologist colleague in Los Angels, says her clinic is full of twenty-four-year-old women who have been speaking in vocal fry for a decade and have developed serious vocal issues.

**Inflection:** The pitch movement over the entire sentence is inflection which helps to make your message clear. An audience gets information in two ways: from the meaning of the individual words themselves and from the inflection. For example when speaking of two contrasting ideas, items, or products, which we do all the time in professional settings, the listener needs to hear a large pitch change from one idea to the next, to recognize that a comparison is being made. The inflection communicates the meaning.

One of the reasons **upspeak,** the raising of pitch at the end of declamatory sentences, is so discouraged in professional settings is that it weakens the message and the speaker. A woman sounds as if she is unsure and asking for approval. There is an exercise below that addresses this tendency.

**Falling Inflections:** Rampant in our culture, falling inflection is the dropping off of pitch, volume and energy toward the ends of sentences. We all do it and it weakens our message, makes us sound uncertain and does not inspire buy-in. There is an exercise below that will help you identify this habit and put a new one in its place.

The following exercises will help expand pitch range, release more varied inflection and counteract both upspeak and falling inflections. They are fun, quick, and can add zest to a warm-up. Do these in the middle of your warm-up, after the voice has been motoring comfortably. Work at a moderate effort level, stay loose and easy.

## Exercise: Ng Siren

1. On the "ng" sound, make a tiny baby or puppy whine, repeat easily several times.
2. Stay on "ng" as you begin to siren in ever expanding loops of pitch – high-ish to low-ish, easing your voice into higher and lower places. (Thanks Gillyanne Kayes for a "ng" siren)
3. Change to an "eee" siren, again in loops of pitch that go from high-ish to low-ish notes. Remember soft knees, long back of neck, soft front of neck and breath.
4. Change to an "ooh" sound, letting pitches swoop and glide. You might, at this point, want to add movement, as the pitch goes up the body goes up, and as the pitch goes down the body goes down.
5. Expand to any vowel, any pitch. Be extravagant as you explore swoops and glides, and let your body follow. There is no right or wrong, just enjoy the pitch and body moving together.

## Exercise: High/Low

Below are two lists of contrasting words. The first word in each pair inspires a higher note. The second word feels as if it needs to be spoken on a lower note. Physicalize, letting the body go up as pitch goes up and down as pitch goes down. Have fun, do this with flair!

| | |
|---|---|
| High | Low |
| Light | Dark |
| Sweet | Sour |
| Happy | Sad |
| Success | Failure |
| Laughter | Tears |
| Friend | Foe |
| Love | Hate |
| Joy | Sorrow |
| Generous | Miserly |
| Tickled | Tormented |
| Freezing | Melting |
| Healthy | Sickly |
| Rich | Poor |
| Reward | Punish |
| Win | Lose |

When you have said the entire list, go back to your vision statement or 60-second pitch and let the inflection go where it wants to go. You should hear some new inflections which feel authentic and natural. No one wants to hear you deliberately striving for pitch and inflection variety. It should sound natural and easy, not calling attention to itself.

Say the above list again, reversing or mixing up the words in the right hand and left hand column, so you are not always going from high to low. This time truly infuse each word with meaning as well as changing pitch. Go immediately back to your own speech. Is your authentic inflection getting clearer and easier?

## 📹 #9 Expanding Pitch Range:

**Exercise: Pitch Absurd**

1. Speak your introduction, vision statement or 60-second elevator pitch and let the pitch move up and down extravagantly, randomly, using pitch extremes, regardless of content or meaning. If moving physically a bit helps you and your voice stay released, then move as well.
2. When you have done the whole speech in pitch absurd, find natural alignment, release knees, keep back of neck long, breathe, and just say the words, letting the pitch go where it naturally wants to go.

**Optimum Pitch**

Optimum pitch is the note around which our voice is the clearest, easiest, most efficient, and resonant. Learning to use optimum pitch in professional speaking situations is one of the best things you can do for vocal expressivity, health, and efficiency.

Many of my clients panic a bit when they find that their optimum pitch is higher than they think it should be. They don't want to sound like little girls. I then demonstrate the power of resonance. I can speak at my optimum pitch without full resonance and indeed sound like a little girl. When I engage the full complement of resonators, at the same pitch previously used, I sound like a woman with a clear, easy voice. In the last chapter, I spoke about the prevailing sentiment that a lower voice is preferable. Speaking below optimum pitch stifles expressivity and vocal variety. Many women attempt a lower voice by lowering the larynx which is not vocally healthy. Speaking at optimum pitch with free and open resonators will always give you more vocal options and be less taxing.

---

**#10 Optimum Pitch: Pringles Tube; 1-10 Shoot for the Middle**

---

What follows are four ways to find your optimum pitch and strategies to help you integrate optimum pitch into your professional voice.

**Exercise: Pringles Tube** (for this exercise you will need an empty Pringles tube)

1. Hold the Pringles tube (without the lid) gently between your thumb and fingers and bring it close to your mouth, almost but not quite touching your lips. Vocalize into the tube on an "ah." Starting at your lowest comfortable note, going slowly up one note at a time. Give the sound

a moderate energy and volume level. Four or five notes up you will feel a vibrational change in the tube. When you reach your optimum pitch, the tube will vibrate in your hand, and you will sound noticeably louder. Not magic – the tube is a biofeedback tool that amplifies your optimum pitch; it feeds back to you your most resonant sound.

2. Once you find your optimum pitch, speak your full name on that pitch, "My name is… and this is my optimum pitch." If you lose it, go back to the tube and find it again. Once you can speak your name at that pitch, try a few sentences of your 60-second pitch or vision statement. Go back to the tube as often as you need to.

3. Find your optimum pitch and speak your entire vision statement or 60-second pitch. Be aware of how it sounds and feels.

**Exercise: One to Ten, Shoot for the Middle**

Count out loud, one to ten, speaking the odd numbers high-ish in your range, the even numbers low-ish in your range. Keep the back of neck long, front of neck soft, don't lead with your chin. Once you have counted to 10, without thinking, planning or judging, shoot for the middle and speak a few lines of your vision statement or 60-second pitch. It should sound and feel similar to the results from the previous exercise.

**Exercise: Five from the Bottom**

Find you lowest comfortable note, vocalize on "ah" and move up five notes. That should be your optimum pitch. Say "My name is… and this is my optimum pitch." Try a few lines of a speech.

## Exercise: Uh-Huh

A quick way to access optimum pitch, is to find your authentic "uh huh," the second note of which is usually your optimum pitch. I use this one sometimes when I am doing voice-over work and I feel my pitch is sitting on the bottom of my voice. I need to bring the voice back to its "sweet spot" quickly. I speak an "uh huh" and the second note of that is my optimum pitch!

A final word about optimum pitch. Though we call it optimum pitch, it does not mean this is the only pitch from which to speak. Think if it as your "center note," with pitches above and below. It is the note around which you will find ease of natural inflection that communicates meaning.

## Curing Falling Inflections

Falling off the ends of sentences is a serious problem for many speakers. It is a usage habit that can be quickly cured with a couple of simple techniques. These exercises let you naturally feel the lift and the forward moving energy from thought to thought. Do these exercises as many times as it takes until your body learns this lesson. Use your 60-second elevator speech.

## Exercise: Toss the Ball

Hold a tennis ball in your hand. On the last word of each sentence, toss the ball up (<u>on</u> the word, not after).

## Exercise: Kick the Box

Put an empty cardboard box on the floor in front of you. <u>On</u> the last word of each sentence, kick the box (kick with a moderate effort level so you are not bashing the box against the wall).

## Exercise: Point the Final Word

As you say the last word of each sentence strongly point with your index finger as if to accuse. Do this for the entire speech. When you are done, go back to the top and try your speech again without the toss, kick or point and see if your body remembers how to lift the end of sentences in an authentic way.

## Exercise: Master Thespian

Another range-extending exercise is "Master Thespian" which, like "Pitch Absurd," encourages the speaker to be extravagant vocally and physically. It is inspired by an old Saturday Night Live skit in which Jon Lovitz and John Lithgow dressed as ambitious, egomaniacal Shakespearean actors, overacted outrageously, voicing and physicalizing in a broad, stereotypic way, mocking acting styles of that period.

- Using your introductory statement, vision statement or you 60-second elevator pitch, try out "Master Thespian," with my permission to totally overact. Use extravagant physicality, pitch range, and vocal qualities. When you have finished the entire speech, find natural alignment, ground, center, breathe and say the speech again, allowing it to be whatever it is, as influenced by the previous exploration.

## Reflective Journal:

Describe how your pitch range reacted to these exercises. What are the changes you noticed? What places in your range seemed to be more comfortable and flow more easily? Did any parts feel creaky or unnatural? Consider the work you did with pitch range, optimum pitch, "Pitch Absurd," and "Master Thespian." What discoveries did you make about your habitual use of pitch and pitch range? How is your optimum pitch different from your habitual pitch? How does it feel? Where, specifically, do you feel the changes in your voice? What questions were raised? What discoveries did you make? How can you integrate this new knowledge into your daily practice?

_____
_____
_____
_____
_____
_____
_____
_____
_____
_____

### *Voices from the Field*

*Young women today have this question mark at the end of what they say. It drives me crazy. I don't think they recognize how invalidating it is, how undermining. It is not cute, not strong. It doesn't give you the credibility that you are seeking.*
*Felicia Collins Correia*

Diana Morgan leads her Toastmasters chapter.

# Chapter 8
# Articulating for Ease and Clarity

**"Language holds power. When it's filled with confidence and passion, and backed up by authentic presence, it can transform us...Declarations create and clarify vision for ourselves and others...It doesn't matter where you are on the path to leadership... declarations make leaders...People who boldly put themselves out there are more interesting, memorable, and charismatic. They exude presence. We admire their pluck and daring. We orient ourselves differently around them."**
Kristi Hedges[1]

The words you choose and how you say them are a crucial part of owning your authentic voice. Think of the most dynamic leaders you know. They use language vigorously; and we respond! Each word is carefully chosen and fully articulated. Dynamic language has **muscularity** and **space**. By muscularity I mean the lips, teeth, tongue and soft palate come together and move apart with energy and specificity – articulation. By space I mean the mouth is open wide - remember the megaphone image in Chapter 6.

It might be helpful here to look at why clarity and energy of language are such challenges for presenters, speakers and leaders. The casual nature of contemporary culture leads us to casual speech. With casual speech comes a mouth that doesn't want to open; thus, vowels are not given ample space and consonants are weak to the point of non-existence. If we are using "contemporary casual speak," the articulators – lips, teeth, tongue, and palate – don't want to come together in an energized way; they approach each other but don't really want to shake hands, as it were.

115

If our habit is to use language in casual or sloppy ways, it will feel very foreign, self-conscious and even awkward to use the articulators with more energy. But if our goal is to transform an audience, make that sale or convince the board that your idea is valid, we must use our articulators in a more athletic way. The exercises below will help you push beyond your comfort zone and develop new and more effective ways of using language in your professional speech.

Let me get on my soap box for a moment about dialect. English is the language of business in this country and in many places throughout the world. General American is the dialect of English spoken in the US by some professionals. But this does not imply that General American is more proper or standard while other dialects are somehow less proper or sub-standard. If you have been given feedback that you can't be understood, you can reduce or "neutralize" your dialect with the help of a dialect coach. I don't feel, however, that everyone needs to speak the General American dialect, how boring would that be! Be proud of your dialect. It reflects where you come from and who you are. Our goal, as we do the work in this chapter, is to gain flexibility, ease, and clarity, so we can be easily understood in professional situations.

Energetic, dynamic speech starts with articulation. That is the clear formation of vowels and consonants as the articulatory surfaces of the lips, teeth, tongue and palate come together and move apart within the space inside the mouth. In this chapter we will practice these skills:

- Articulation of vowels and consonants
- Flexible, responsive articulators
- Clarity of thoughts

Western spoken languages are made up of two major sound categories: **consonants** and **vowels**. In the General American dialect alone there are twenty-three consonants and nineteen vowels and diphthongs. These sounds are literally made all over the mouth, and the mouth needs to be working harder for professional speech than it typically does for social interactions. Through awareness and practice, these sounds will become more specific, clear, and emotionally engaging.

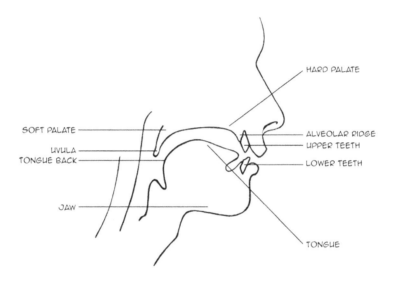

In the illustration of the speech organs above, you will notice the articulators which include the lips, teeth, tongue, palate, soft palate and uvula. Each of these needs to be exercised and sensitized to the specificity required for clear speech.

**Consonants**

Consonants give language energy, clarity and definition. Defined, a consonant is an obstruction of air flow. As we learned in chapter 4, as air flows out on the exhale, the vocal folds vibrate against the airflow, creating tiny puffs of disturbed air. That stream of air is then obstructed in some way by the articulators and we have created a sound we know as a consonant.

## Exercise: Consonant Exploration

1.  Using a small hand mirror, look at your mouth:
    Look at your **lips**. Bring them together, making a popping noise as they come apart. Say **p**, **b**, **t**, **d k**, **g**. Try **p** and **b** several times, energetically bringing the lips together and feeling them fly apart with the force of the breath. Look at your mouth in the mirror as you make these sounds. Try **t** and **d**. Notice the tongue touches the alveolar ridge to make those two sounds. What parts of the mouth come together to make a **k** or a **g** sound?

2. Try **f**, **v**, **s**, **z**, **sh**, **ch**. Make each sound several times, energetically bringing the lips, teeth and tongue together feeling the energy of the air hissing through.

To build strength and flexibility, repeat the following sounds several times, feeling the energy of each sound. Be sure to breathe!

3. puu tee kaa, puu tee kaa, puu tee kaa, puu tee kaa
4. buh dah geh dah, buh dah geh dah, buh dah geh dah, buh dah geh dah

**Consonant Drills**

Repeat the following phrases several times at a low volume level (too much volume on consonant drills can cause unwanted tension). Remember to check in with natural alignment, deep breath and space in the mouth. Use optimum pitch, rather than letting the voice sit down and back on the vocal folds. Enjoy the full energy of the consonants, particularly final consonants. Really wrap your mouth around them, using more muscularity than you normally would. These are fun to do. Memorize the ones you most enjoy and use them as part of your personal warm-up.

1. Unique New York, unique New York, you know you need unique New York.
2. Big black bugs brought buckets of Black Beard's blood.
3. Red leather, yellow leather.
4. My mother makes marmalade to make Marv merry.
5. A skunk sat on a stump.
   The skunk thunk the stump stunk
   And the stump thought the skunk stunk.

6. Let us go together to gather lettuce
   Whether the weather will let us or no.
7. Five frantic fat frogs fled from fifty fierce fishes.
8. Cheryl's cheap chip shop sells cheap chips.
9. If a hair net could net hair,
   How much hair could that hair net net,
   If a hair net could net hair?

## Exercise: Mouthing

Going back to your 60-second elevator pitch, "mouth" the entire speech; that is, really use the articulators, but make no sound. Fully engage the lips, teeth, tongue, hard palate and soft palate, as if you want a person across the room to read your lips. When you have completed mouthing the entire speech, speak the text on voice, paying as much attention to the articulators as you did when you mouthed.

## Exercise: Every Part of Every Word

With the same speech, at a low volume level, slowly pronounce every part of every word, every tiny syllable, every middle and final consonant. When you have finished the entire speech, speak at normal pace and volume level.

## Vowels

I chose to start our speech discussion with consonants, but of course that is only half of the picture. Vowels are the other branch of clear and expressive speech. If consonants are the bones of speech, then vowels are the heart and soul. Some say that while consonants carry the clarity of meaning, vowels impart the emotional content. Both vowels and consonants must be fully realized for speech to be clear to the ear and piercing to the heart.

Vowels are created by unobstructed air flowing through an open mouth. We change vowels by changing the shape of the mouth.

Let's look first at long vowels. These are vowels that sustain sound for a period of time.

> *ee* as in e̲at
> *ah* as in f̲a̲ther
> *oo* as in g̲o̲o̲se

## Exercise: Long Vowels

Try the long vowels, repeating each several times with energy. Explore pitch, levels, and length as you fully experience each vowel before moving on to the next.

> *ee* as in e̲at
> *ah* as in f̲a̲ther
> *oo* as in g̲o̲o̲se

## Exercise: Short Vowels

In contrast to the long vowels, short vowels are quicker in duration.

> *i* as in ki̲t
> *uh* as in stru̲t
> *u* as in pu̲t

After you have said the vowel within the context of the sample words above, isolate each short vowel, feeling its quick, incisive energy.

Diphthongs are two vowels that are spoken as one sound. There are five in the General American Dialect. As you speak the words below, pay close attention to the underlined diphthongs, feeling the blending of the two vowels to form one.

> *ay* as in f<u>a</u>ce
> *i* as in pr<u>i</u>ce
> *oy* as in ch<u>oi</u>ce
> *o* as in g<u>oa</u>t
> *au* as in m<u>ou</u>th

## Exercise: Diphthongs

Explore the diphthongs repeating each several times with energy. Explore pitch, levels, and length as you fully experience each vowel before moving on to the next.

## Exercise: Vowels Only

1. Using your vision statement or 60-second pitch, speak only the vowels and diphthongs, eliminating all consonants. Do this easily, letting the vowels flow one in to the other. Don't worry about getting each one perfectly in order; speak the essence of the vowels, using a kind of "soupy," free-form modern dance rendition. I find it helpful to move with this exercise, so everything is kept free and open. The focus is on carving out the space in the mouth for the vowels.

2.  When you have completed the speech in vowels only, find natural alignment, let the breath settle, and speak entire speech. Be aware of what has happened to the vowels as a result of the exercise.

**Exercise: Clarity of Thought**

After the consonants and vowels have been worked and your articulators are warmed and energized, the next step is making each thought clear.

1.  Say your speech as if you are thinking each word as it comes out of your mouth. Each word was chosen by you for a reason. You need to fully breath, make space in the mouth and enjoy each word.
2.  Give yourself the strong intention to be clear enough so a listener could take notes on what you are saying.
3.  Finally, release it and trust that the work you have done on muscularity and specificity will be there, you don't have to think about it. Your body just does its job, so you can focus on the effect you are having on the listeners.

**Record your Speech**

Thanks to the convenience of smart phones, you can easily watch and listen to yourself work. I know you can overcome being self-conscious about this and can learn to watch and listen to yourself objectively. You will hear when words are not clear, when you are falling off at the ends of sentences. You will catch those fillers "uh," "um," "like," "ok." They are easier to banish when you actually hear them yourself.

**Always warm up your articulators before any presentation, whether speaking to one person or to a group.** Use any of the exercises above or create your own, but it is mandatory that you make articulation a part of your daily warm up.

**Reflective Journal:** Now that you have learned about consonants and vowels, how they are defined and how they are formed, describe how your understanding and awareness of the specificity of sound have deepened. How did it feel to use more muscularity in your own speech? What exercises were the most effective for you? What will you take on as part of your personal practice?

_____

_____

_____

_____

_____

_____

_____

_____

## *Voices from the Field*

*It is important for a women to realize a lot of work gets done outside the work day in social settings. I was just in a meeting talking with a local developer about some concerns he had and a third gentleman walked in. Looking at the developer, he said, "Let's get that other guy in on a meeting. Why don't you set up a thing for the three of us to have a beer and let's just work through this." He did not include me in that scenario. I just said, "That is a great idea, let me know when. I'd be happy to join you for a beer." Women need not be afraid to insert ourselves firmly and clearly in those situations. If we are left out of these conversations, relationships are made, promotions happen and we will still be sitting at our desks.*
       Kathy Taylor

Rena and Estela release jaw tension.

# Chapter 9

# Communicating Through Body Language and Movement

"As I live, I express my life-force in movement; as I move I feel my aliveness...Where movement is both free and integrated, there life will be felt to flow freely and strongly."
Linda Hartley[1]

"Your body doesn't know how to lie. Unconsciously, it telegraphs your thoughts as you fold your arms, cross your legs, stand, walk, move your eyes and mouth."
Julius Fast[2]

"There is nothing more attractive than a person with shining, sparkling, fully present eyes...Eyes with a light in them show life, energy, awareness and a reflection of a physically, mentally and spiritually healthy person."
Meribeth Dayme[3]

Michelle Obama is a superb example of an authentic, skilled speaker who makes a connection with her audiences, both large and small. When she walks on the stage, there is no doubt that she owns it – she is at home, easy, relaxed and fully present. Notice her natural alignment, her confident stride, her grounded and centered stance. Before she even opens her mouth, we know from her body language that we are in capable hands. David Oats, President of Stalwart Communications observed, "While Mrs. Obama used prepared remarks, she presented them with genuine sincerity and emotion. She believed in what she was saying and the audience got that. She was confident, not cocky...she had her eyes on people, not prompters...Instead of focusing on the screens, Mrs. Obama made sure she engaged the people in the hall at a personal level."[4]

Another reason for Mrs. Obama's physical and vocal ease is practice. Her level of mastery does not happen by accident; she knows how to prepare. And she has been in front of people a lot, for many years before she became First Lady. I can't emphasize enough the importance of putting yourself out there. Each time you do, you learn and improve. Even if it is terrifying, you must step up, risk, and even fail a little, in order to grow. (See Chapters 2, 4 and 5 for exercises on taming performance anxiety and building confidence.)

Let's start from the premise that the body is always communicating. How you move through space, how you stand, where you carry your weight, where you focus your eyes, how you use your hands and the tilt or lift of your head communicates something about you to your audience. Even the smallest details of physicality tell viewers volumes about each of us, leading them to form opinions, both positive and negative. The body speaks its own story, apart from our words. Though specific studies differ on the actual statistics, it is safe to say that well over half of what an audience knows and understands about us is derived from our body language. It is ironic that many speakers may spend hours writing and practicing a speech and then just hope the body will come along for the ride. Esteemed leadership coach, Kristi Hedges says, "…your actions underline or undermine your presence."[5] In order to ensure that our body works *with* us rather than *against* us as we speak, this chapter will explore unique ways of understanding how the body works. We will look at some large and profound truths about how the body is organized to create meaningful communication, as well as some details about how to manage and use the body to tell compelling and convincing stories. We want our body's story to become just as deliberate and conscious as the story we tell in words.

To get your body ready for easy, confident movement and gestures, you need to warm it up by loosening and freeing, releasing habitual tension as described in Chapters 2 and 3. Attend to each body part, starting with head, neck and moving through the entire body, stretching, shaking and breathing.

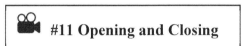

**#11 Opening and Closing**

**Exercise: Opening and Closing**

This exercise will help you feel the difference between an open body and a closed body. Think of "openness" and "closedness" as a continuum - moving from the most open to the most closed. In this exercise we will move back and forth slowly from open to closed, allowing you to experience sensations in the body and at various points on the continuum.

1. Start in natural alignment. Be aware of the breath in your center.
2. Widen your stance to shoulder width, and extend your arms above your head so you are standing in a giant X. Extend your arms and feel the energy coming from the floor up your body and out your hands, breathing deeply into your center as you do this. Be aware of how this feels throughout the body.
3. Now round over, curling yourself into a small ball, holding your muscles tight, closing yourself. How does this feel?
4. Then extend into your giant X again, feeling power, openness, breathe deep into your center.
5. Curl into a ball, closing yourself again.

6. Go back and forth between open and closed, at your own pace, 8 more times.

7. Return to natural alignment: feet hip width apart, knees soft, pelvis balanced, spine easily lengthening, head floating on top of the neck, chin parallel to the floor, shoulders relaxed and down, and breath dropping into your center. Hopefully you feel easy strength and relaxed confidence. This probably feels similar to the grounding and centering exercise from Chapter 1. This physical state should become your base line, your default. Whenever you speak, present or pitch, this is where your body starts.

## The Right Amount of Movement

I am often asked "How much should I move?" "Do I move too much?" "Is it boring just to stand there?" No matter what you do physically, stay grounded, centered and open. If you feel compelled to move or gesture, make sure it reinforces what you are saying. Movement trumps word. A listener will always follow gestures over the spoken word; so random movement quickly becomes distracting. When it comes to gestures, less is usually more.

It is my hope that after doing the exercises outlined in this chapter you will start to feel comfortable using gestures. When I am coaching speakers who truly don't know what do with their hands, I will choreograph a few telling gestures and encourage practice until they feel natural. You can also keep your hands relaxed at your sides, resting on the podium, or easily holding your notes.

If you use your hands a lot, make a video of yourself and watch the playback. If you are moving your hands all the time – simplify. Pick the gestures that communicate something specific and stick with those. Ask a friend to watch your presentation and give feedback about gestures. Encourage them to be honest and specific.

If we are not consciously aware of our hands, they will do what the body needs; they will reveal our inner emotional world. If emotions are open, hands are open. If emotions are closed, hands are closed. If you release habitual tension and do some opening and closing, you will start to feel more confident and comfortable and your hands will begin to look more comfortable as well.

## Pacing

Some speakers are always on the move. If that is you – stop. It is more important to remain grounded and centered than constantly moving. If you are in front of a medium to large group you may want to think of your movement pattern in terms of a triangle. Center front is the starting point. If you have a major transition in the subject matter, you can take several steps to the right or left and find a new person to talk to. Then stay put for several sentences. On another transition or subject change, you can look to the other side of the room and take a few steps in that direction. Then stay put until the next transition which takes you back to center. You have made a movement triangle. In a five-minute speech, one pass of your triangle, or three movements, is all that is necessary. Major movement comes at thought shifts only. Gestures are used to reinforce a point, to illustrate or enhance energy – never just because you don't know what else to do.

At your next presentation ask a friend to video your speech. Watch it later and be honest with what you see. You will notices what habits or mannerisms are effective and which are distracting. Recently I watched the recording of one of my presentations and I noticed how many times I adjust my scarf – I no longer wear scarves when I speak. I also became aware that I habitually tuck my hair behind my ears – I now spray my hair back so I won't be tempted to play with it. Your goal is to be the best you can be, learn from your mistakes and make changes. But don't punish yourself or dwell on your mistakes, just notice, practice and grow.

## Eye Contact

Eye contact is a crucial part of being fully present and building true rapport. When presenting to a group, pick one person to look at for the length of a sentence, then pick out another face to speak to for the length of the next sentence.

Some speakers use the 180-degree-eye-sweep, which takes into account the full view of the room through your peripheral vision. This is a good way to establish the comfortable limits of your eye contact range. The danger here is it can give unconscious permission for your eyes to sweep from one side to the other without ever really seeing. Eyes that truly see faces establish rapport and connection.

In one-on-one conversations, eye contact moves naturally to the other person and then away. I try to give eye contact when the other person is talking. When I am talking, part of the time I give eye contact, part of the time I gaze away to find a new thought. Observe the use of eye contact in the conversations around you to see how natural eye contact works. We can get hints about how to use our own bodies by observing how others use theirs and seeing what is effective and what is distracting. Excellent speakers and presenters are dedicated observers of life around them, always watching for how people use their bodies, their gestures, and their eye contact in real life when they are not self-conscious.

If eye contact is a real issue for you, or if you have been given feedback that you need to do more, I encourage you to ask a trusted colleague or family member to observe you and take notes about the presence or absence of eye contact. When I coach clients, I will ask them to look at me, use me as a real audience member. "Tell that to me." Or I stick "post it" notes at three or four spots on the wall and ask the client to speak to the spot as if they were faces in the audience. You can do this for yourself – practice your speech with awareness for eye contact.

Some speakers have a habit of looking at the floor to get their next idea. Know that anytime the audience loses your eyes, they lose connection. When you are gathering your thoughts or thinking about what's next, use a sightline slightly above the heads of the audience to refresh your next thought.

Before we progress to specific types of gestures, film yourself practicing a speech, a "pre-test" look at your body language.

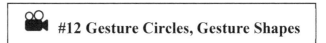

**#12 Gesture Circles, Gesture Shapes**

## Gesture Circles

My dear friend and movement specialist colleague Matthew Ellis shared an image with me that has proven invaluable as I begin to talk body language to clients who have not done much physical work. He talks about the body in terms of three sections or circles of energy. The first circle is our lower abdomen, where survival instincts reside, where sexual energy is centered, where need for food and shelter take root. The second circle includes the stomach, heart and lungs where tenderness, love, vulnerably, hurt and loneliness are housed. Finally the third circle includes the throat, mouth, brain where our intellect, words, and sense of humor are focused. All authentic movement or gestures come from the body, from an impulse or a need that originates in the body, specifically from one of these three areas or energy centers.

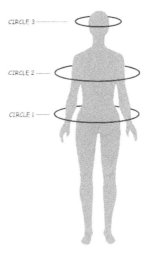

In Circle 1, if I am talking about base instincts, survival, deep fear, a violent act, my center of energy will be lower in the body, and a gesture will also remain low at my waist and closer into the body. Observe Jade in the next illustration.

If I am speaking of love, disappointment, compassion, my heart center is activated and my gestures will be at chest height. I am gesturing from circle 2, as Jade is doing in the illustration below.

In Circle 3, if I am speaking of something I know in my mind to be true, or I want to appeal to the listener's intellect, my gesture is going to be closer to my head, mouth or throat, as Jade shows us below.

**Exercise: Gesture Circles**

Create a set of three gestures that feel comfortable for each circle. Link them to a sentence or phrase.

> Examples:
> "She did as you would do, she fought to protect her child." Circle 1
> "Your heart must break when you hear these details." Circle 2
> "Please think before you decide." Circle 3

Create phrases that you might actually use in a speech, presentation or pitch.

Then explore a gesture that goes with the phrase. Practice speaking and gesturing at the same time. If you discover one you believe might work for you, even if at first it does not feel natural, repeat it over and over until it does.

Film yourself, you can tell if a gesture looks natural and adds to your message.

## Gesture Shapes

Gestures also have shape in space – triangle, square and circular. A triangular gesture shoots out from the center like an arrow, is attacking, accusing or directing attention toward. "He did it." "She sits there before you." "It started with her." "That one over there."

The square is immovable. "This is the situation," "Let me explain it this way." "For our purposes today."

Circular is taking and giving back. "This is for you; this is for me." "All of us are in this together." "This is true both before and after."

**Exercise: Gesture Shapes**

1.  Practice a triangular gesture for the following phrases:
    "I would not be here today if not for her."
    "You, my friend, are wrong."
2.  Practice a square gesture for the following phrases:
    "All of the evidence leads to this conclusion."
    "What I offer here will save you time and money."
3.  Practice a circular gesture for the following phrases:
    "You buy a pair of shoes; we give a pair of shoes."
    "This process is on-going."

Go back to the video you made earlier as you examined your movement patterns. Watch it again, observing how you use gestures in light of this new information.

Choose a gesture you observed in the video. Is there room to clarify and sharpen, making the body circles clear and more dynamic? Practice the gesture as you say the sentence. Repeat several times.

Go back again to your video. Focus on gesture shapes. If you point for any reason, are you pointing with clarity and conviction? Is there an opportunity for a square gesture? Pick a sentence and try a square gesture. A circular gesture is probably the most challenging. You may want to reinforce consequences ("as a result," "in order to," "if you do that – this will happen"), or the circular nature of a relationship ("first you, then we" or "this builds on that"). That kind of language cries for a circular gesture. If you identify words that are similar to these examples, try a circular gesture.

Think back to when you learned to ride a bicycle, or first took up golf or tried to perfect your tennis serve. The first 10 attempts were probably pretty rough. You may have felt awkward and uncoordinated. But if you persisted, your parent let go of the back of the bike and you pedaled forward, or your club made solid contact with the ball, or you hit the serve gracefully over the net! As adults mastering body language, we may want to give up the first time a movement feels awkward. With practice, though, these movement concepts can be mastered and the physical map of your presentations can be award-winning.

**Reflective Journal:** What do you notice in terms of your movement? Your gestures? Eye contact? Where do you look relaxed? At what point do you look uncomfortable? Which gestures support and reinforce what you are saying? Are there any that are distracting? Can you eliminate the ones that don't add to or support what you are saying? In light of the information regarding gesture circles and gesture shapes, what do you see in your own gestures? Are you using the three gesture circles? Do they match up with your choice of language? Which gesture shapes do you use most frequently? Are there opportunities to employ other gesture shapes?

_____
_____
_____
_____
_____
_____
_____

## *Voices from the Field*

*Eye contact has been especially important to me. I often speak to large groups of twenty-somethings, and I find I keep their attention best by varying my pitch and vocal patterns and making brief, pointed eye contact rather than sweeping the room with gaze.*

*Anna Fearheiley*

*I was in an international meeting with a Japanese CEO I had just met. He started by saying, "Ok Teri, tell us something about yourself." And in my big Oklahoma accent I started talking. And beside me, the CFO interrupted me mid-sentence, "I can see your mouth moving, but with that accent I have no idea what you are saying." It was total silence. And in my head I am thinking this is a defining moment. And I turned to him and said, "Not to worry, you'll figure it out." Everybody laughed and that changed everything. I didn't take it personally, but I had to say something. I owed it to myself; I couldn't be a wallflower in this position. My humor and a touch of sarcasm worked. I also knew I needed to be prepared; my intellect was important. Ultimately I won them over as they recognized that I had an authentic desire to help them.*

*Teri Aulph*

Estela Hernandez shares her passion for education.

# Chapter 10
# Perfecting Your Personal Mission Statement

**"It is vital to take ownership of your message, your platform, and deliver it with authority. Avoid imitating anyone else, just work and practice to be the best "you" you can be. I get excited and passionate about my topics so I am always working on my voice and keeping hand gestures simple and clear."**
Cecilie Croissant

As I recall the people I have encountered who most eloquently and passionately spoke their personal mission, I am reminded of mentors whose lessons have stayed with me through the years - Allan Sterrett, Ron Willis, David Carey and Jane Boston. All are educators, artists and masters in their fields who are on fire to effect change in the hearts and minds of their students. They each possess clarity and dynamic confidence in the truth of their personal mission statements, honed by years of tireless repetition.

I was in Allan Sterrett's English class at Amphitheater High School, in Tucson, Arizona, when we got the news that Martin Luther King, Jr. had been assassinated. He wept as he told us who this man was and the universal significance of his life and death. Mr. Sterrett introduced me to Shakespeare, the Romantic Poets and Charles Dickens. He not only opened doors of opportunity, he pushed us through, forcing us to see the world as so much bigger than ourselves.

Ron Willis, on the faculty at the University of Kansas, had a huge personality, enormous intellect and wit, and he was always teaching. In his booming, resonant voice, he told me the directorial choices I was making were superficial, "You are capable of so much more, dig deeper." And I have been digging deeper ever since.

David Carey, who I referenced in Chapter 4, was head of the Voice Studies program at London's Royal Central School of Speech and Drama. He is a subtle, generous, highly ethical, well-read, gifted voice and text coach who told me in our first tutorial, "You work a bit hard don't you." He went immediately for the soft underbelly of my deepest fear – that I would never be good enough unless I worked harder than anyone else. I still work too hard, but at least now I fearlessly own it. What I learned from David is the concept of "power without press." He was always powerful, focused, disciplined and authentic but he was never forced or pressed. David's lesson to me, mastery through ease, is one which I am still learning and hope to pass on through my work with women.

As I reviewed examples of noteworthy speakers of the personal mission statement, I realized that there are no women! How can that be? Especially since now my life's work is to empower women? Then I look up from my computer and see a picture of Jane Boston and me in New York City, toasting the publication of our book, *Breath in Action*. That glass of wine marked the end of a seven year journey that started on the train from Brighton to London.

Jane was a lecturer on the voice course at Central and I was totally taken with her clarity, understated passion and depth of knowledge. After I completed the program, I had this idea that Jane and I needed to write a book together, though I had little to contribute as a fledgling voice trainer, but I knew I could learn so much from a collaboration with her. So I pitched the idea in an email.

Jane responded by saying she didn't really have time to talk about it but she did take the train every day from Brighton, where she lived, to London, where she worked at the Royal Academy of Dramatic Art. If I wanted to ride the train with her, we could talk about it then. So I took the two hour train ride to Brighton, stayed the night in a bed and breakfast, met Jane at the station the following morning and rode the train with her. By the time we got to London, we had agreed to write, in her words, "a little book about breath."

As it turned out I contributed a lot in terms of organization, research, communication with authors around the world and tenacity. We published our first book. Jane's gift in taking that journey with me was perhaps the greatest of my life – she showed me I could take on a huge international project and wrangle it to completion.

All these amazing mentors have one thing in common - they all could passionately tell their stories. They lived their personal mission statements every minute of their professional lives. And they could articulate their missions authentically and persuasively. Anyone who wants to advance, grow, be heard or make a contribution must learn to do the same.

Part of our work together will be the writing of your mission statement, and of course practicing so you can stand and deliver! It will be meticulously rehearsed and yet feel totally spontaneous. You will learn to use your authentic voice to tell the world who you are and what you stand for.

**Reflective Journal. Write the answers to the following prompts:** This does not have to be great writing. Don't censure yourself. Just write.

What are the important roles you play in your life?

_____
_____
_____
_____

Where do you find your deepest sense of satisfaction?

_____
_____
_____

What activity makes you feel complete?

_____
_____
_____

Where do you find your "zone?" What are you most comfortable doing?

_____
_____
_____

What issues do you care most passionately about?

_____
_____
_____

Why do you feel you were put on this earth?

_____
_____
_____

What would you like to be written on your tomb stone?

_____
_____
_____

## Write your Personal Mission Statement

Read your answers to the questions above. Feel free to add thoughts, ideas and responses not covered in the questions. Your life, your passions and your mission are unique to you. Look for the common themes, words or activities. Write down whatever thoughts occur to you, without editing. Some years ago, when I first started writing, I found a book called *The Wild Mind: Living the Writer's Life* by Natalie Goldberg. Her recommendation is to write this phrase, "What I really want to say is…" Write it again and again until your subconscious begins feeding you words. It allows you to go to a deeper level, to connect with what is really going on inside. Turn off your inner critic and write from your heart. You can always go back and revise it later. Draft a version of your personal mission statement.

_____
_____
_____
_____
_____
_____
_____
_____
_____
_____
_____
_____
_____

———————————————————————————
———————————————————————————

**Exercise: Working with your Personal Mission Statement**

1.  Read your mission statement out loud just to hear the words. Don't worry about *how* you say it yet, just say the words.
2.  **Warm up.** If you have not already warmed up the body, take a few minutes to release physical tension, soften the knees, connect with deep central breathing, create long back of neck and soft front of neck, release the jaw and tongue, lift the soft palate and expand your pitch range.
3.  **Breathe your speech.** This time through, focus on breathing at each punctuation mark. Find the moment of readiness at each new breath, the moment the inhale becomes the exhale. If you find you are running out of breath before the end of the sentence, find a place to logically take a breath that does not interrupt the flow of a thought. Read it all the way through for breath only. Let your body learn where the breaths are. Just as you memorize words, so the body memorizes where the breaths happen.
4.  **Your mouth is your megaphone.** This time focus on space in your mouth as you read. Make bigger space for all the vowels, particularly the long vowels and the diphthongs. LOVE the vowels!
5.  **Bite the apple.** This time as you read, use the image of biting the apple to lift the soft palate. Refresh the sense of space on each new breath. It will be louder and the resonance will feel more forward in the mouth.
6.  **Consonant muscularity.** Speak it softly at a low volume level, focusing on consonant energy, especially final

consonants. Feel the activity on your lips, teeth and tongue. This helps you build articulation clarity. After you have read the entire speech for consonant energy, speak it normally.

7. **Read it in tongue speak.** Really let the tongue hang all the way out; don't try to project. Then just say it again with your tongue back in your mouth. It will be easier to say and clearer!

8. **Circle all the nouns.** Nouns are the most important words. Anything you can point at - a person, place, a thing - is a key word.

9. **Point out the nouns.** As you read this time, point your index finger on each noun as if you are pointing out the object. Do this with energy and fully extend the arm, hand and finger; feel energy through the tip of your finger. Be aware what this activity does to those nouns.

10. **Circle the action verbs.** As you are reading, toss a tennis ball in the air each time you say a verb (you can also use the finger point, if you don't have a tennis ball).

11. **Read your statement again.** Do the nouns and verbs have a little more life, energy or specificity?

12. **Cure falling inflection.** As you read this time, energetically point your finger <u>on</u> the last word before each punctuation.

13. **Do the "ee" siren, 1-10, Pitch Absurd or Master Thespian.** Shake up your pitch range and inflection. Be bold, have fun and don't hold back.

14. **Final read!** Repeat your statement one last time, letting the inflection just go where it naturally wants to go. You should be getting close to the final, presentable rendition!

This is your free, expressive voice, supported by an aligned body, adequate breath support, resonance with space in the mouth for vowels, and clarity of articulation. The expressive voice has endless options for pitch and inflection variety. It is a voice that believes it has something to say.

Each time you practice, go through these steps. It may feel like it takes too much time, but I guarantee the results will be worth it. There really is no shortcut to perfection. To be the best you can be, you have to work the process.

### Voices from the field

*Very early on, I noticed how frequently women would precede their contribution to a debate with "I'm sorry." Things like "I'm sorry, it's just that I think…" or "I'm sorry, but I wonder if…" It was a striking difference from our male colleagues. Even though I wasn't particularly prone to it, from time to time I would catch myself about to use this little crutch. It was like sticking a foot out to catch a door before it closes, to give yourself a chance to squeeze in. There are plenty of things I have to be sorry about — when something sad, hurtful or disappointing happens or I feel for someone, or when I've disappointed someone or been a jerk — but having an opinion about our strategy, work or approach isn't one of them. It's part of my job — a big part — and I'm not sorry about doing my job and working with my team. I made a point of reserving "I'm sorry" for those situations that really, really call for it. In removing this conversational crutch from my toolbox, I became clearer in the verbal expression of my opinions, and more creative in how I held my own while still being open, inclusive and friendly on the job.*

*Jessica Reading*

Rena and Shay polish her candidacy announcement.

# Chapter 11

# Refining your 60-Second Elevator Pitch

**"The words you use when you are talking define how you think about yourself. Give me a few minutes of conversation with almost anyone and I'll be able to tell you whether that person thinks of himself or herself as a champion or a chump…If your verbal message sounds like a perpetual whine, you must expect that people will treat you accordingly. If you speak with authority people will react to you as a person of authority. If you speak words of love, people will react to you with love. If your words reflect seething anger, don't be surprised if people avoid you – or enlist you in their battles with someone else."**
Steven Brown[1]

Since the creation of Vocal Authority, I have attended two to three networking luncheons weekly. I also belong to several professional organizations whose functions are advocacy, education and networking. Part of the agenda of these meetings is an opportunity for each attendee to give a short 30-60 second commercial about who they are, what they do or what problem they solve, to spark curiosity or start a conversation.

The term "elevator pitch" comes from the imagined scenario that you find yourself on an elevator with the boss, the decision maker, or a new colleague and you have the time from the closing of the door to its opening on the destination floor to pitch who you are, what you contribute or why you'd like to have a meeting. You have seconds to communicate your message and catch their attention with clear confidence, without bluff or denial.

In order to take advantage of these spontaneous opportunities, you must be prepared. You practice so you can be spontaneous.

Of the hundreds of 60-second pitches I have witnessed, a small percentage were very good, many others not so much. Where do they go wrong? Let's make a list of characteristics of the "pitch gone wrong."

- Most people try to wing it. They stand up and hope that the right words come out. Usually they don't.
- They are peppered with fillers like "umm," "uhh," "OK."
- They don't breath.
- They don't open the mouth.
- They speak too fast.
- They speak too softly.
- They are terrified and their nerves show.
- They don't making eye contact.
- They end with an embarrassing tag, or they just taper off into nothingness.

By contrast, let's look at the characteristics of the speaker who delivers the 60-second "pitch from heaven."

- They have carefully written it to reflect exactly what needs to be said and they have practiced it – a lot.
- Because they know what they are going to say next, they don't have to fill the silences with "umms" or "uhhhs."
- They breathe deeply at each punctuation.
- The open their mouths.
- If they are truly breathing, they won't talk too fast.
- If they are breathing and making space, they will be loud enough.
- If they have been breathing deeply through the previous pitches, their nerves will be under control.

- They actually make eye contact and *see* the people they are talking to.
- They don't taper off at the end.

What are situations or circumstances in your life where you might need a 60-second elevator pitch? A networking meeting is only one. In a sales situation you have a matter of seconds to open the door of opportunity to speak in detail to a prospective client. At parties, you may want to introduce yourself succinctly and authentically. You have a great idea for a new process or product and you need to explain it to the decision maker before her attention shifts to other matters. What if you had 60 seconds to advocate for a raise or a promotion, what would you say? Would you be clear and confident?

In this chapter you are going to write and rehearse a 60-second pitch which is appropriate to your needs or situation.

**What elements should your 60-second pitch contain**? (Does not have to include all. Use this list as guideline only)

- Your name.
- Your business, position, contribution, or proposal.
- What is the problem that you, or your proposal, solves?
- Benefit statement: How people have benefitted or will benefit from this?
- A specific example (people love stories).
- What is unique about your business or proposal?
- Conclusion: can be a summary, restating name and position, inspiring quote, or ask a compelling question, "Are you ready to...?
- Use a clever tag only if it is a really good one and doesn't sound "salesy."

**If you are searching for a job, consider such words as:**

- Adept at…
- Proficient in…
- Accomplished…
- Prowess…
- Dexterity…
- Expertise in…
- Savvy…

**If putting forth an issue, consider such wording as:**

- Because…
- On behalf of…
- I owe it to…
- I'm inspired by…
- I want to inspire…
- I believe…

**If selling a product or service**: consider using personal emotional needs of potential clients

- frustrated
- concerned
- disappointed
- losing sleep

**Write in your Reflective Journal:** Use this space to write a new version of your 60-second pitch

_____
_____
_____
_____

_____
_____
_____
_____
_____
_____

**Prepare to practice:** Once you have written out word for word, warm up the body and voice. Before you begin speaking, attend to each of the following:

**Exercise: Warm-up**

1. Release of habitual tension for ease.
2. Find natural alignment, grounded and centered for presence.
3. Engage deep central breathing.
4. Make space for resonance: lengthen back of neck, release jaw and tongue, lift the soft palate.
5. Pitch Range for expressivity, ee siren.

**Exercise: Practice your 60-second pitch**

1. Read it out loud to check out the words.
2. Breathe your speech, breathing at each punctuation.
3. Read it in tongue speak.
4. Bite the apple, to lift the soft palate.
5. Open your mouth for the vowels.
6. Engage consonant muscularity by mouthing
7. Point out the nouns.
8. Circle the action verbs.
9. Point your finger on final words to avoid falling inflections.
10. Do the ee siren, 1-10, Pitch Absurd or Master Thespian.

11. Repeat your statement one last time, letting the inflection just go where it naturally wants to go. You should be getting close to the final, presentable rendition.

**Record your practice.** Film your 60-second pitch. Watch yourself, notice when you can't be heard, when you are not clearly articulating, or making space in your mouth. Are you using filler words or are you dropping at the ends of sentences? Are your nouns and verbs specific and clear? Does your body language enhance your message?

**Before the actual presentation:** A few minutes before you go into your meeting, warm up your body and your voice. Keep your performance anxiety under control by engaging slow deep breathing. As others are speaking, continue to focus on your own deep breathing.

When it is your turn to speak, stand to full natural alignment before you start to speak:

- Find your feet.
- Soften your knees.
- Breathe.
- Make space.
- Speak.
- Make eye contract.
- Breathe at each punctuation or change of thought.
- Maintain vocal energy until you have finished your final word. If you are new to the group restate your name and the name of your company.

Finally, ask for feedback from the team leader or a trusted friend. If you are invested in being the best you can be, feedback is an important tool to judge how you are progressing. A great speaker is always in "beta," testing, revising and growing.

### *Voices from the field*

*In my work, sometimes I have to deliver negative feedback. Criticism can be hard for women. My supervisor recently gave me feedback that I am too intense and candid on conference calls, and people sometimes think I'm angry. Although it was hard to hear, I took a step back, processed it and ultimately adjusted my approach. That kind of feedback helps us grow. We need to understand how our interaction impacts others so we can be better. Women need to be more open to that. There is nothing wrong with getting your feelings hurt; feel however you are going to feel. We can't decide how we are going to feel about something, but we can decide how we are going to react to it. Make mistakes and learn from them. It's all part of the evolutionary process of being strong women!*
     Cheena Pazzo

*I have been holding leadership development seminars, teaching and encouraging people to use public speaking as a tool to advance their careers, to showcase their expertise from the stage. After these sessions, I have conversations with women who are fighting with that insecurity about putting themselsves forward. Some of it is basic nervousness. Some of it is worrying about their skills, their competence level, and their credibility. Second guessing themselves with the question, "Do I belong at a podium instructing others, sharing my knowledge?" I have a client who is a bank executive, highly knowledgeable, who worked her way up through the ranks, and has a wonderful story to share. I was amazed at how nervous and resistant she was to share all that from the stage. It was fascinating to watch her work through it.*

*Early in my career I became aware of the need to manage the number of words we have to say. Women have more words*

159

*than men. In any given day we speak about 10,000 more words than men do. I can remember times as a young professional when I suddenly became very conscious of the fact that, "You have been speaking for a very long time." Every once in a while I still have to catch myself, "That's a lot of words! You need to bring it home." We, as women aspiring to leadership, are not always aware that we can learn to manage that.*
    *Aurora Gregory*

*I encourage all women who aspire to leadership to read and study continually about any and all topics that interest them in order to develop a good vocabulary and knowledge about several different areas that pertain to their position or goals. I encourage woman who want to speak before large audiences to get mentoring in correct vocal use and other areas that pertain to their position. Avoid imitating anyone else, just work and practice to be the best "you" you can be. Additionally, it is vital to take ownership of your message, your platform, and deliver it with authentic authority. As a woman I have spoken all over the world. In certain countries, a few people literally left the room when they realized that a woman would be speaking. In other countries, I was well received. One middle-aged woman remarked, "You preach like a man." It was not meant as criticism; it simply was an observation on her part that I spoke with passion, boldness, and conviction, and she was not used to seeing that! She actually opened the door for me to speak to all the women in her district. I tend to get pretty excited and passionate about my subjects, and I am learning to use my voice properly and also avoid having too busy hand and arm movements. I want to come across with clarity, conviction and professionalism. I try to bring value to others in everything I do. People who are sincerely open for what I have to share will respond well, and those who are not open, well, I am just not that worried about.*
    *Cecilie Croissant*

Shay White shares her story of resilience with her voters.

# Chapter 12
# Voicing Leadership

**"The ability to be comfortable with a pause is central to gravitas. It says that you trust yourself; that you are not desperate to please or to fill a silence. In a moment of silence you understand the truth of the old acting rule that the most powerful person in the room has the most relaxed breathing pattern."**
Caroline Goyder[1]

As I reflect on the leaders that I have directly encountered in my professional life, both male and female, I first hear a warm vocal quality, a measured pace, an ease of body and a command of language carefully chosen to tell the narrative. I think of the actress Jane Alexander. As chairwoman of the National Endowment of the Arts from 1993-1997, she spoke with warmth, authentic power and confidence as she advocated for federal funding for the arts. She was grounded, centered, and comfortable in her own skin. I remember feeling comforted by the sound of her voice, like we were in the most capable of hands.

One of my dearest friends Ruth Brelsford, an award-winning educator, has a voice and presence that takes over a room in the best sense of that image. She speaks with a deep sense of personal truth; she has a well-trained voice that is warm and resonant, possessing confidence born of years in the classroom, directing for the theatre, and political advocacy. When Ruth speaks, everyone listens.

I am also reminded of David Boren, former Governor and Senator, currently President of the University of Oklahoma, who I had the privilege of hearing speak many times during my fifteen-year tenure at that university. He spoke from the heart, using emotionally evocative stories to highlight his themes. He celebrated people he encountered in his career who inspired him for any number of reasons. Even when I heard the same story repeated (yes, he recycled) I was often moved to tears. His formula is simple - start with a personal story rich in detail and generalizes outward to the universal truth he wants to reinforce. His tone is folksy, having been raised in Oklahoma, but not overly so; he sounds authentic to himself. He makes a personal connection to each audience member even in a stadium filled with graduates and their families.

Let's look at how the elements we have already discussed in this book apply directly to leadership. A great leader is physically at ease, comfortable in her own skin. A body that is fraught with tension will never move with ease. Even if a leader has physical issues which hamper ease of movement, she can maximize the range of movement she has by easy release exercises of stretching and shaking (Chapters 1 and 2).

The leader has easy natural alignment – feet hip-width apart and weight evenly distributed, knees soft, long back of neck, shoulders relaxed and down. Her arms and hands rest easily at her side, until they are activated by a specific need to gesture (Chapter 3 & 9).

The quote that opens this chapter reminds us that the most powerful person in the room has the most relaxed breath. As you enter the space, breathe slowly and deeply. As you prepare to speak, breathe. Continue to breathe deliberately at each punctuation mark in your speech. Breath allows you to find a measured pace and gives you freedom to pause for dramatic effect. You will not feel the need to fill silences with umms, errs or uhhs; breath fills the space, allowing you to consider what comes next. Your deep breaths allow the audience to relax and breathe with you (Chapter 5).

You remember that a warm quality and compelling tone of an effective leader is created through resonance and enhanced vibrations, which come from space in the mouth (Chapter 6). You remember to lengthen through the back of the neck, release the jaw and tongue, and lift the soft palate. Compelling leaders have expressive voices that move easily through their pitch range. In addition to natural inflection, you are aware that inflection communicates meaning.

Building on the vocal and physical techniques you have already been exploring, let's focus on how to apply these directly to leadership situations that demand more of the voice than our personal mission statements or 60-second elevator pitches. There are also three new exercises that I have saved for "Voicing Leadership:" the Two Finger Drop, Radiating 360 Degrees, and Action Verb Images will help stimulate variety.

What kind of messages are you called upon to deliver in your work environment?

- Explaining and justifying policy change.
- Sharing your company's story or philosophy for employee morale and buy-in.
- Unveiling a new product.
- Advocating for legislative policy.
- Summing up for the jury.

Choose one that pertains to your situation or create a topic uniquely suited to your needs.

**Write your speech,** thinking about the following points:

- Introduce yourself and your topic: How will you get immediate attention and interest? What relaxes you and allows you to be authentic? Why are you excited to be here?
- Outline your goal or what you want to accomplish in your speech. Perhaps briefly outline for your audience the points you intend to cover – lay out your plan.
- Develop your points paragraph by paragraph.
- Add stories that provide detail, evoke emotion or add humor.
- Include quotes from other speakers or writers that add emotion, meaning or context.
- Create transitions between points, connecting the dots from one thought to the next.
- Summarize what you have covered.
- Thank your listeners. End with a final inspiring thought.

**Use your Reflective Journal to write your speech:**

_____
_____
_____
_____
_____
_____
_____
_____
_____
_____

_____

_____

_____

_____

_____

## Exercise: Practicing your Speech

1. **Read it outloud.** When you have finished writing, read it out loud to see if you have a created a speech you can actually say. We often write more formally than we speak. We need to write like we talk – simply, clearly and authentically.

2. **Warm up** your body and voice so you can bring your best to your practice.

3. **Breathe your speech.** As you read out loud, breathe at each punctuation, sensing the moment of readiness. This not only teaches you where to breathe, it helps you find the natural pace and keeps you grounded and centered (Chapter 4).

4. **Use the two finger drop.** To help you rehearse space in your mouth, speak one sentence with two fingers in your mouth – actually talk around your fingers. (Ever see the movie _The King's Speech?_ That voice coach used a bone prop to keep the King's mouth open – your fingers are your built-in bone prop.) Then speak the sentence without the fingers while remembering the space that your fingers created. Alternate this sequence sentence by sentence through the entire speech.

5. **Mouth the speech.** Without sound, wrap your lips around each word as if you want a listener to read your lips. Then speak it focusing on clear and easy articulation.

6. **Eliminate falling inflections.** Point that index finger firmly forward on the last word of each sentence. Or kick a box or toss a ball.

7. **Sing your speech.** If you enjoy singing, you will love this one. Just pretend you are an opera singer or a torch song balladeer and make up a song. Don't think about it – just sing! Then speak the speech and enjoy the ease of natural inflection and phrasing you found as you sang.

8. **Become a Master Thespian.** If singing is too far outside your comfort zone, try Master Thespian. Ham it up as much as you can, both physically and vocally. Then say the speech and just let it be what it wants to be.

## Presence: Owning the Room and Radiating 360 Degrees

We have already explored presence and owning the room (Chapter 1 & 5). You recall that it starts with being grounded and centered, as you feel your feet firmly connected to the floor and your knees soft. To get centered, feel that your energy source is located in the area of your navel. You are breathing deeply and centrally. Your shoulders, neck and head are released. You are making easy eye contact. Your level of performance anxiety is low and your level of joy is high.

Highly successful speakers, leaders and politicians have something extra often called **charisma**. They seem to radiate warmth, confidence and energy. You can learn to radiate warmth, confidence and energy – in all directions!

**Exercise: Radiating 360 Degrees**

1. Stretch each rib cage, patting the ribs to encourage deep release.
2. Find your feet, soften your knees and feel long back of neck, soft front of neck.
3. Connect to a deep central breath by finding abdominal release.
4. Release your jaw, lips remain gently closed.
5. Feel energy and focus coming out through your eyes, as if your eyes have laser beams. Don't squint or try too hard to manifest this feeling. Just feel that your eyes illuminate whatever you are looking at.
6. Shift the focus of your attention to your center, imagine that energy is flowing from your center. You have a super power that is housed in your center. With each breath it gets stronger. Your eyes and your center radiate warmth and confidence.
7. Now send your focus to your back. Imagine that you can breathe in and out through your back. Then picture a group of supporters that stand behind you, giving you strength. You don't need to turn your head to see them; you sense they are there – your breath and your radiating energy can touch them.
8. Speak a few sentences and imagine your voice easily flowing out your back to the supporters who stand behind you.
9. Bring awareness to your rib cage. Feel each inhale expand the ribs. Bring awareness of space into the ribs cage. Imagine that your rib cage is aglow with energy.

169

Your superpowers are not just in your center and your back, but also in your ribs.

10. Speak again and feel your ribs radiate with sound energy.

11. Imagine a glow of light all around your body – a thermographic image. As you breath feel it becoming stronger and clearer. Be sure you have not picked up tension in your knees, shoulders, upper chest or jaw.

12. Say your speech again, imagine that your whole body is an amplifier; sound comes out all around you, managed from your center. Don't let tension creep into your knees, shoulders, neck and jaw. Continue to breathe deeply and make space in your mouth.

**Explore Body Language and Physicality**

Whether movement comes easily or is challenging for you, film your speech to see what your body is doing. Are you moving too much? If so, reign it in by creating an easy triangle traffic pattern discussed in Chapter 9. If you are not moving at all, is there a transition where you can move a few steps to the right or left? If your speech is several minutes long try to find at least two places to move.

Look at your gestures. Do they clarify your message? Match word choice with gesture circles (Chapter 9). If you are talking about base instincts of fear or survival, are you gestures lower, near your waist? If you are speaking of love, devotion, or loyalty, are your gestures just above your waist, nearer your heart? If you are appealing to the intellect, are your gestures higher, near your head?

Look at the shape of your gestures. Do you use triangular, square or circular gestures? Are there opportunities to try a new gesture that might clarify a point? Find a place for one of each gesture shape and practice until it becomes natural.

**Use Action Verb Imagery.** What effect do you want this speech to have on your audience? What is your intention or objective? Do you want to inspire? To scare? To accuse? To warn? To comfort? To empower? To coax? Having a clear intention in mind will help you intensify the emotional effect your words will have on the audience. Don't just choose the intention, breathe it in. As you are practicing deep central breathing, breathe in the need "to inspire," for example. Feel it deeply and then say the words.

If your speech is 4-5 minutes long or longer, you will want to assign several action verbs to different sections. The first section could be "to inspire," the second section "to warn," the final section "to empower." Write your action verb in the margins. These images will inspire you to find different tones, rates and volume levels which will lend variety and interest to your speech.

**Make eye contact.** When I practice a speech, I place objects or chairs in my rehearsal space to give me something to focus on, as if I am looking into the specific eyes of audience members. If in my practice I allow my eyes to glaze over, the same thing will happen when I am in front of an audience. Performance is a result of remembered rehearsals, so practice as you want to perform.

**Note Cards and Beyond.** So far we have only worked from fully-written scripts. Ultimately you will put that aside and speak from remembered talking points, key ideas or images. From a full script, make an outline and practice from that. If you want to go without notes, try creating a visual map of your journey through your talk. Visualize the first point, see it in your mind's eye. What pictures come next and next?

**PowerPoint.** If you use PowerPoint in your presentation, don't talk to the screen. Glance at it to get your next thought, then give eye contact back to your audience. You are the important part, not the screen. Don't stand in the dark. Put the screen to one side, make sure you are visible, and look at your audience. It is your energy they will remember, not the information on the screen. We have all witnessed PowerPoint presentations done poorly. Practice as if a screen is beside you.

Ultimately these are all practice techniques. When you actually speak you want to release the work and focus on what you are saying, trusting that all the preparation you have done will sustain you. Techniques are only useful if they help free you to be your best authentic self. Remember to breathe as you wait in the wings, breathe as you walk in, find your feet, soften your knees, feel long back of neck, breathe into your center and speak from your heart!

After your presentation, celebrate what you did well, and acknowledge what still needs work. Let yourself off the perfection hook. The leader in you is always a work in progress.

### Voices from the field

*I was working with my non-profit advisory board - a group of men - and we couldn't get off first base in terms of how to structure the fund raising pitch. I couldn't figure out what was happening. I finally said, "OK guys, when we go to make the pitch, you have to tell me if it would hurt or help for me to go with you? We are asking for money from these folks and I don't know how they feel about African*

*Americans, if that is going to get in the way. It is not about me; my self-esteem is not wrapped up in how other people see me. The bottom line is getting the donation. If you tell me it would not be a good idea to go – I won't." I named the issue, the elephant in the room. Once they knew we could talk about it, they wanted me on every call.*

*Sometimes with race issues, I have to use humor. That seems to work – it neutralizes the environment. I grew up acutely aware that I was an anomaly. I knew in order to get people to pay attention to me, I was going to have to work at it. In school, I always made top grades. At the beginning of each school year my mother would still have to demand that I be placed in the class with other top performers – they wanted to put me in the "B" group. They wouldn't or couldn't acknowledge the implicit bias. I grew up knowing there was not going to be parity and fairness and I was going to have to create it.*

*When my husband and I first moved to Tulsa, his friends remarked, "Your wife is a rough assignment." I wasn't sure what that meant so I started paying more attention. When there was a gathering, the women would be together in a group and the men would be in another group. I noticed I would drift over to where the men were. If they were talking politics I would contribute to the debate; I would give my opinion. That was unusual to them. I grew up with three brothers, and a strong mother – that was my world. To me, if I wasn't attacking the big issue, what was I doing? If I saw a problem – teen pregnancy prevention, infant mortality – I called it out, "There is disparity of where you live and the outcome for your baby." If I didn't say it – who else was going to? It was unconscionable not to.*
    *Felicia Collins Correia*

Rena and Kendra enjoy building a rousing political speech.

# Chapter 13
# Running for Office

**"At a conference we moderated at the State Department, former U.S. Secretary of State Hillary Clinton spoke openly about the fear she felt when she decided to run for the Senate in 2000, after eight years as First Lady, decades as a political spouse, and a successful legal career. 'It's hard to face public failure. I realized I was scared to lose,' she told us. That caught us off guard. 'I was finally pushed,' she said, 'by a high school women's basketball coach, who told me, 'Sure you might lose. So what? Dare to compete, Mrs. Clinton. Dare to compete.'"**
Katty Kay and Claire Shipman[1]

I have been politically engaged my entire life. My parents were both involved in grass roots, precinct-level activities, so I grew up intrigued by the political process. Today, in our highly charged nation, where everyone has an adamant point of view, women are more crucial than ever in leading and moderating the debate. Women's natural tendencies to maintain relationships, build consensus and multitask uniquely equip us to make significant contributions in local, state and national politics. In addition, women office holders tend to be more actively involved, responsive to constituents and advocate more for gender-salient issues."[2]

As of this writing, there are 21 women serving in the United States Senate (21%) and 83 serving in the House of Representatives (19%). According to the National Democratic Institute (NDI), at the current rate of progress, political parity won't be achieved until 2080.[3] Even with these disappointing statistics, there has never been a better time for women to step forward and run.

Hillary Clinton, Elizabeth Warren, Kirsten Gillibrand, Maxine Waters, Lisa Murkowski, Kelly Ayotte, Claire McCaskill, Kamala Harris and others are making their voices heard, paving the way for more women to run.

There are numerous reasons, however, why women choose not to run for office. We are less likely to think we are qualified to hold office. We are less competitive and more risk adverse by nature. And finally, we still bear the majority of the responsibility of raising children and maintaining households.

If you are one of the brave women who has decided to step forward and run for public office, your voice is your best tool for getting your message across to voters. I am currently coaching a savvy young woman running for a state house seat. Our work together has opened her eyes to the art of using the voice in conscious and specific ways to make her speeches more authentic, clear and dynamic.

For her work, I have added "Owning Words." As a politician, she wants to rouse and engage her voters – get them fired up. So that she remains authentic and grounded, even as her energy level rises, she needs to fully understand and feel the key words more deeply - own them at a "gut level." She pictures each important image, sees it, breaths it, says it several different ways until she has a real connection with the word, before moving on to the next. This moves the center of the energy from the brain to the belly so the speaker and the audience have an authentic experience of the word.

We will also look at the importance of lists in political speeches and how to build them toward the applause. And remember, the applause is for *them*, more than for you, as it drives their enthusiasm up and deepens their emotional connection to you and your message.

In addition, the foundational work of breath, grounding, confidence, body language outlined in the previous chapters are imperative to take on board daily as you ready your speeches.
You will need a 60-second, a three minute and a five minute version of your story: who you are, what you are running for and your three top issues – your stump speech. If you are given five to ten minutes, add personal stories that tell listeners about yourself and what inspired you to run. Also develop stories about why you have chosen your top issues. Be as specific as possible. Details deepen the audience's emotional responses to your story. Avoid jargon. Use plain speech. Don't use a big word when a simpler word will do. Finish with your name and a request for their vote.

**Reflective Journal:** Write out a version of your stump speech.

_____

_____

_____

_____

_____

_____

_____

_____

_____

_____

_____

_____

_____

**Now practice, practice, practice** until it feels natural and easy. It will get more and more authentic and dynamic, if you follow the preparation process outlined below.

## Practicing Your Stump Speech.

1. Warm up the body to release tension (Chapter 2).
2. Fully warm up the voice – "T'ai Chi," "The Archer" (Chapter 6).
3. Warm up your pitch range (Chapter 7).
4. Ground and center, feeling your weight evenly distributed over both feet.
5. Revisit the Internal Space Awareness exercise (Chapter 2).
6. Connect with your breath, finding the moment of readiness. (Chapter 4).
7. Feel long back of neck and soft front of neck.
8. Be aware of space in the back of the mouth (Chapter 6).
9. Breathe your speech. Say your speech out loud, breathing at each punctuation. If you didn't give yourself enough punctuation, add some. You should speak no more than seven to nine words on a single breath. The audience needs you to breathe, so they can breathe, relax and actually listen to you. Your deep breathing will also help you stay calm and keep you from speaking too fast. Under pressure we often tend to race. It is okay to pause to breathe and gather your next thought. Rehearse several times, waiting for the "moment of readiness" in the breath (Chapter 4).
10. Read your speech again making space for the vowels. Open the mouth, more than you think is necessary. Make your megaphone as big as you can. Continue to breathe at punctuation. Revisit the "Two Finger Drop" or "Vowels Only."

11. Explore consonant energy by "Mouthing" or by using "Every Part of Every Word" (Chapter 8).

12. Owning words. Circle the key words – nouns and verbs. In the following exercise you will learn how to "own" each of them. I want you to really feel them in your center and imagine a vivid picture of what each word means.[4]

13. Speak each word that you have circled out loud by itself. Repeat this several times, in different ways, until you have an image of what that word really means to you. What do you see when you say that word? Fully realize it. If you want the audience to feel the impact of the word, *you* must see it and feel it as well. Work through each circled word in this manner. Put the speech back together and notice if your key words matter more, if you are taking more time with these words, and if you are indeed "owning" them.

**Lists.** Political speeches often contains lists. "I am for this, this and this." Our challenges are there, there and there." "First I will address this, then that and finally this other thing."

Lists need to build, which will help you increase the audience's excitement. The build will signal to the audience that it is time to applaud. Think of stacking the list up the wall. The first item is low near the floor, the next one is a foot higher, the third is a foot higher still, and the final item is as high as your shoulder and the final item is as high as your head.

14. Physicalize as you speak the list up the wall. Get the feeling of the build in your body. With your hand actually mark the place on the wall where each item would be. Allow your voice to gain energy with each

new mark up the wall.[5] Put the list back into the speech and see if you can keep the authentic build that you felt as you physicalized up the wall. Don't force, let it happen naturally.

Put the list back into the speech and see if you can keep the authentic build that you felt as you physicalized up the wall. Don't force, let the build happen naturally.

15. **Point up final words:** To avoid falling inflections, point your index finger on the final word of each sentence. Speak it again without the finger and see if you can maintain forward energy to the end of the line.

Audiences love variety and change. Change can be found in rate, inflection, volume, energy or body language. The moment when something shifts, the audience pays extra attention. When more than several sentences are the same, audiences tend to tune out. I encourage the discovery of transitions through exploration. The exercise that follows will stimulate the voice and body to organically find new paths.

**Finding variety with action verbs.** The use of strong action verbs that define the effect you want to have on an audience can help you find variety. If I were to ask you "to warn the audience," your voice and body would make adjustments in order to accomplish that. If I were to coach you "to inspire the audience," your body and voice would change in rate, energy level and inflection patterns in order to achieve that. Good verbs for political speeches are: to comfort, to celebrate, to implore, to defend, to inflame, to cajole, to console, to inspire, to motivate, to activate, to shame, to horrify, to pray, to plead, to scold, to tease, to preach, to lift up. You get the idea.

## Exercise: Action Verbs

1. **Assign action verbs to each paragraph:** Divide your speech into topics, thought groups or paragraphs (whichever makes the most sense to you). Assign an action verb, from the list above, to each section of your speech. Write it in the margin. Those verbs become your road map through the speech. Read the speech allowing the verbs to inspire your voice and body. Explore these in an extravagant way; you can always pull it back.

2. Ground and center, connect with your breath, and say the speech, allowing the verb images to guide you through. Be particularly aware of the moments when change or transition happen.

## Exercise: Shake it up

1. You have now done a lot of exploration with your speech. Through each rendition, your body has learned something about how to present these words. The last step is to shake it up by dancing it, singing it, doing "Pitch Absurd" or "Master Thespian" (which ever of these exercises appealed to you from Chapter 7).

2. One more time find your feet, soften your knees, let your breath settle, and just say the speech, letting it be what it authentically wants to be.

## Exercise: Film your Speech.

- **Film your speech.** Focus on your body language. Do your gestures look comfortable? Do they support what you are saying? Is there an opportunity to fine tune gesture in terms of gesture circles and gesture shapes

(Chapter 9)? Are you moving too much? Do you need to ground your feet and simplify?

Running for elected office requires a great deal of effort: raising money, organizing your campaign team, distributing yard signs and knocking on doors. All require time. But your most important asset – you and your message – must take precedence and cannot be short-changed. The process I have outlined takes time, but it will place you in a far better position to actually reach your goal – to win!

**Media Interviews**

One of the most anxiety-inducing aspects of running for office is the media interview. It is free flowing, containing unknown variables that need to be reacted to in the moment. Inexperienced politicians often find this daunting. There are a few strategies that you can adopt which will stabilize you, giving you a greater chance for success. (Special thanks to the Carl Albert Congressional Research and Studies Center: Women's Leadership Imitative and the Oklahoma's Women's Coalition for assembling this excellent information on media interviews.)

First, decide what your message is going to be, what your goal is for this interview. Pick two to three main points. Rehearse them!

- Thirty to sixty minutes prior to the interview, do your warm-up. Begin focusing on deep central breathing. Review your main points. Allow enough time to get to the venue so you don't have to rush.

- Continue to breathe slowly and deeply as you walk into the interview space.

- Ground your feet, soften your knees, and think long back of neck, soft front of neck.

- Listen intently to what is being asked of you. Look the reporter in the eyes. Think carefully about your response, and breathe before you speak.

- Don't fake an answer. If you are asked a question that is out of your area of expertise, admit it.

- Don't say "no comment." If you truly can't respond, explain why and bridge to a point that you want to cover.

- Don't go "off the record." Everything you say to a reporter can end up "on the record."

- Don't feel the need to fill silence. Say what you want to say and stop. Keep breathing through the silence.

- Don't lose your cool – keep breathing deeply, especially if you feel anxiety rising.

- Tell the truth.

- Make sure you know what commonly used acronyms stand for. Use the full name of the association or committee at least the first time you mention it.

- Take control if bullied. Keep breathing deeply and remain calm and unintimidated. This can help you regain control of the interview.

Watch out for these traps:[6]

- False Facts: If a reporter quotes incorrect information, ask for the source of the facts. Politely say the information is incorrect and bridge back to your point.

- Hypotheticals: If you are asked to respond to a forecasted event, say "I don't want to speculate," and bridge back to your point.

- Interrupter: If the reporter does not let you finish, stop, listen patiently to the questions and then say, "I'll answer your question in a moment, but I'd like to finish my first answer."

- The Paraphraser: If a reporter incorrectly restates what you said, restate your position by saying, "I guess I didn't make myself clear…"

- Loaded question: If a reporter only gives you two options for an answer, you can say, "There are other choices…"

- The bombshell: If a reporter accuses you of say "dropping the ball," don't repeat negative language. Replace, saying "I wouldn't use those terms…What I would say is…"

One of my favorite episodes on the TV series *The West Wing*, was "Debate Camp." You and your team can hold your own "debate camp" of sorts to help you prepare for the interview. Brainstorm possible questions, both easy and challenging; write them down on separate pieces of paper. Give a question to each team member. Have them ask the questions as if it were a real interview situation. Practice your response. Video tape your mock interview. You and your team can look at the playback and offer suggestions and comments. Through practice you will gain confidence and ease with the media situation.

After you have done all of your homework, then release yourself to speak from your heart. Trust that the foundation you have laid through practice will support you. Don't be afraid to be passionate. If you are grounded in the breath, you will find the appropriate amount of energy, and you will be neither too much nor too little. You will be just right. You are enough!

**Reflective Journal:** What are your strengths as a candidate? What areas do you need to shore up? What aspects of political speaking inspire or excite you? Which aspects cause you fear? What ideas presented in this chapter were new to you? What points are you going to carry forward into your daily practice?

_____
_____
_____
_____
_____
_____

## *Voices from the field*

*When considering a run for office, there are a lot of factors to keep an eye on – nonverbal signals, tone of voice, how you speak – all are crucial. Women are still held to a different standard than men, how people react to you is going to be different, how you get people on your side is going to be different. Women have to prove themselves to be competent; men are assumed to be competent. Women have to be perceived as likeable. Studies show that people will vote for a man they don't like; they will not vote for a woman they don't like. A woman can't be too soft or too abrasive. It is a tricky middle ground of clearly confident but not too passionate. In men, passion is perceived as leadership; in women, it is preserved as hysterical.*

*As more and more women run for office, other women will be inspired as well, offering more role models of how to be authentic, how to be yourself. The woman who puts herself out there to run for office must first be clear as to exactly why she is running. She must also expect criticism and judgement. It is imperative, then, to be comfortable in your own skin and have a firm grasp of personal strengths. Female candidates must be supremely prepared on every level – the voting history of your district, knowing the residents of your district, as well as being extremely well versed on your issues. Volunteer for other campaigns, get comfortable knocking on doors. Get a lot of practice in front of people. Seek and accept feedback and criticism from friends – build a community!*
    *Kendra Horn*

*The most important thing when you are going into an interview situation is to be supremely clear about your message, your goal. An interview with a media person, reporter, or blogger, is not a conversation. You have to go in with an agenda because the reporter has an agenda. If you are not totally clear on the message you want to get across, you will allow yourself to be lulled into a conversation. The reporter can guide you anywhere. If you are not careful you will lose the opportunity to communicate the two or three most important points that matter to you. Think of the reporter as a conduit. Decide before you go into the interview the two or three things you want to say. Use every question as an opportunity to weave in one of your points. That repetition forces the reporter to use it. You have very little time. You don't get to look at it later or make edits or additions. Once the reporter says thank you – that's it.*

*We need to have role models. Progressing on a political path is both exciting and terrifying. I encourage women to find someone in public life whose style you can appreciate. Make an effort to dissect what they do that you like, or would like to learn to do. We also need to put a lot of effort into learning beyond your own sphere of expertise. That requires observation, preparation and a little bit of bravery. Be curious to learn what is beyond your own desk. As women we are uniquely qualified to build relationships, to nurture and care for our constituency. Women still face challenges even though there has never been a time when we have had so many smart, well-educated, well-informed women.*

*Aurora Gregory*

Kendra Horn asks for your vote as she runs for US House District 5 in Oklahoma City

# Chapter 14
# Caring For Your Voice

**"Many professional voice users –including teachers, clergy, and politicians - do not give much thought to the manner in which they speak, much less take precautions to prolong the life of their voices and to prevent potentially career-ending vocal injuries. Once hoarseness, throat pain, or vocal fatigue occurs, individuals suddenly become acutely aware of the integral role voice quality plays in communication and find themselves scrambling to learn behaviors and techniques to rehabilitate their voices."**
Kate Devore and Starr Cookman[1]

Now that you are better acquainted with your voice through the work we have done so far, you are ready to explore how to take care of it. As we dedicate time and study to using the voice in more commanding and dynamic ways, it might help to have a better understanding of behaviors and choices that effect vocal health.

For most of us, including many professional speakers, the voice is a mystery. Sometimes it works; sometimes it doesn't. Sometimes the sound is all there and it feels great; sometimes it sounds hoarse, husky, shaky or thin, beyond our control. The voice can be understood, taken care of and used in such a way that it is predictable and reliable. The voice should serve you, not undermine you.

You only get one voice in your life. If it breaks, you can't go out a buy a new one. You must know how to care for it to insure that it lasts a lifetime. Learning how to protect those two delicate vocal folds is crucial. Make no mistake, keeping your voice healthy is under your control and it is your responsibility.

How your voice feels and functions is not a matter of chance or genetics; it is a matter of conscious choice and daily attention. If you make large demands on your voice, you should be aware of what the voice needs to stay healthy. If you want to be an effective, compelling sales person, teacher, lawyer, politician, pastor, receptionist or anyone who uses the voice to make a living, you have to start being aware of the things that can damage your voice and a few strategies that can keep it healthy.

If your voice gets fatigued when you speak, if you finish the day with a hoarse or husky voice or your volume is weak, review the good vocal usage habits you have learned in this book:

- Release habitual tension before you speak (Chapter 2).
- Practice natural alignment, grounding and centering (Chapter 1 and 3).
- Breathe deeply and centrally when you speak (Chapter 4).
- Make space in the mouth (Chapter 7).
- Speak at optimum pitch (Chapter 7).

If you always use good vocal production habits, your voice will always be strong and flexible.

In addition to vocal usage habits, there are a few life-style adjustments that can make a difference.

**Get plenty of rest.**

Boy, this is a hard one. The voice is one of the first places in the body to feel fatigue and the last place to feel rested. We live in a society that remains sleep-deprived much of the time. We expect our bodies to perform at high levels, often with insufficient rest. However, if you want your voice to be in the best possible shape, the body and the voice need to be well-rested.

In addition to rest at night, your voice needs periods of quiet throughout the day, particularly if you are a heavy voice user. I talk to my clients in terms of "vocal units." This is a metaphor for thinking about the endurance capacity that a voice has throughout any given day. For example, let's say that you have ten vocal units available to you each day. You may use two units in the morning as you shout at your child to get ready for school. You may use two more vocal units as you greet a colleague in a noisy office. Three or four vocal units may be spent cheering at your daughter's soccer game. Then if you have a presentation to make, you only have two units left for a task that may require four. If you use your voice beyond its daily unit allotment, the voice will begin to show fatigue. It may not be as loud, it may sound a bit husky, or you may feel a thickness in the larynx. A little quiet time with a cup of warm tea can feel like a rest to your voice.

Each person's vocal units are different. Some people have voices of steel with a seemingly endless supply of vocal units. These fortunate few are able to use, and even abuse, the voice for long periods of time without any negative effects. Others may fatigue after a lengthy conversation on the phone. You can increase your vocal units with proper usage, lengthening the back of the neck and using adequate breath support. But the concept that your voice has just so much it can give you in a day must be honored if you want to keep the voice healthy.

**Drink plenty of water.**

Water keeps the vocal folds hydrated, which is very important in maintaining general vocal health. Fifty to eighty ounces of water a day is a good estimate, depending on your size. My clients get used to carrying a bottle of water with them all the time. Be especially diligent about hydration both before and after a demanding presentation. A good rule of thumb - you know you are well hydrated if you "pee pale."

**Avoid caffeine, carbonated beverages, acidic juices, milk, and alcohol.**

This is particularly true before heavy voice usage. Caffeine and alcohol are diuretics, draining moisture from the body and from the vocal folds. Milk can causes an increase in phlegm, which can lead to the need to clear the throat. It feels to me like carbonated beverages strip natural moisture from the throat and create gas in the stomach which can surprise a speaker in embarrassing ways. Acidic juices can irritate the stomach which can cause reflux that irritates the vocal folds. Not all people react in the same way to these beverages. You need to know your voice and give it what it needs to operate at optimal efficiency. When in doubt, drink room temperature water or warm herbal tea.

**Avoid talking in competition with loud noises: in subway stations, air planes, noisy parties, or over loud music**.

Talking over noise causes our vocal folds to work harder. We do it unconsciously. My recommendation is to avoid using the voice in these situations. When it is impossible to avoid, be sure that you are using deep central breathing and keeping a long back of neck. Social chitchat and talking on the phone can be great vocal unit drainers as well. Think about your alignment when talking on the phone. Most of us literally let the body cave in on itself, effort goes right to the vocal folds and stays there, as Markeida does in the illustration to the left. A simple adjustment in her alignment, on the right, and she is "good to talk."

**Don't smoke**.

I don't know that I even need to mention this, because most people are aware of the dangers of smoking and more people don't smoke than do. But I am going to stand on my soap box, for young professionals who may be lured by the "sophisticated look" factor. We are all pretty much aware that cigarette smoking causes all kinds of health issues including heart disease, stroke, cancer, high blood pressure, and premature aging of the skin. Cigarettes also have a profoundly negative effect on the voice. Smoking is like cooking the vocal folds. They stay constantly inflamed and are more susceptible to hemorrhage, infection, and swelling. Over time the smoker's voice gets huskier and hoarse, and pitch range diminishes as the vocal folds loose elasticity. Secondhand smoke is equally hard on the voice.

**Avoid screaming.**

Athletic events and shouting at friends over loud music are the two situations where screaming is common. With adequate breath support, length in the back of neck, and space in the mouth you should be able to project the voice at a level that allows you to enjoy the game or be heard by your friends without total laryngitis the next day.

**Avoid pushing forward with the head and neck while speaking.**

It is common for us to extend the head and neck as we speak, particularly if we are intent on making a point. This postural habit, however, shortens the space in the back of the neck, raises the tension level in jaw and tongue, and cuts off the ability to access deep breathing. In both social and professional settings, I can improve my voice usage immediately by keeping length in the back of my neck and breathing a little more consciously and deeply.

**Be aware of certain medications.**

Antihistamines that you might need to take for allergies can be drying. Be sure to drink more water while taking these medications. Avoid throat sprays that numb pain as they can make vocal folds more susceptible to strain, infection, or irritation. Mentholated lozenges are drying to the vocal folds; find non-mentholated substitutes.

**Take care of acid reflux.**

Acid reflux (heartburn or indigestion) can bubble up and irritate the vocal folds, causing you to sound hoarse or husky. If you have regular bouts of heartburn, or feel a constant need to clear the throat, try Maalox or Mylanta and avoid eating heavy, fatty, or spicy foods before bedtime. If it is a serious problem for you, a doctor can prescribe an acid blocker like Nexium.

**Consider a "cool down."**

After a full day of speaking, it is helpful to "cool down" the voice. Try a couple of these fatigue-soothing exercises: Easy humming in the middle of the range, gently humming into your kazoo, or slowly breathing in and out through a straw. Yawn, stretch and sigh out gently on an "ah."
Repeat several times.

If you earn a living by using your voice, I encourage you to follow these guidelines so you can avoid the "scramble to rehabilitate" the voice as described in the quotation that opened this chapter. Prevention is the key!

**Reflective Journal:** Finish the statements below:

With regard to taking care of my voice, what I already do pretty well is

_____

_____

_____

A couple of things I could do better are

_____

_____

_____

What surprised me about taking care of my voice was

_____

_____

_____

Who do you know who has a lot of vocal stamina? How do you compare?

_____

_____

_____

What is your action plan for taking better care of your voice?

_____

_____

_____

Jade Latimer Graham advocates for troubled children.

# Chapter 15
# Polishing Your Warm-Up

**"Cultivate a repeatable process for getting yourself in the zone. Executives can practice these 'pregame rituals' just like athletes do before they take the field...they don't have to be elaborate...it is unique to the person and relevant to that person's intention. Pregame rituals dispel nerves and put you in a positive frame of mind to succeed. An effective ritual also gives you confidence that if it worked once it will work again."**
Kristi Hedges[1]

You have now gone through the entire process of *Empowering Your Voice*! I want to leave you with a final set of warm-ups – a shorthand for continued practice and refinement. Vocal and physical warm-ups are crucial in the life of any speaker, presenter, teacher, attorney, pastor, leader or politician. They are not just a part of training that can be learned once then set aside. Voice work should be done every day. Just as an athlete must work out daily to keep muscles strong and skills sure, so the speaker must keep the vocal and physical instrument sharp, flexible, and toned through daily warm-ups. This chapter offers three sample warm-ups of varying lengths that will sustain you as you build better vocal strength, control, and clarity. Do these with attention and focus. Don't let yourself go on auto-pilot, going through the motions without thought. Be mentally present whether you have thirty minutes or five. Make every warm-up an opportunity to learn something new about your voice, to increase your awareness about yourself.

Ideally, you will develop your own sequence of warm-up exercises that works for you. Each of us is different, and our bodies and voices respond better to certain exercises than to others. Some of the activities presented throughout this book will have worked well for you, and some may have not. Take on the ones that work; set aside those that don't. As you have experienced in the other chapters, there is a natural sequence to follow each time you warm up:

- Release and stretch the body.
- Find natural alignment.
- Get grounded and centered.
- Connect to a deep central breath including abdominal release and moment of readiness.
- Make space in the mouth.
- Wake up vibrations.
- Expand pitch range.
- Energize the articulators.
- Connect words to an authentic need to speak.

Wake up the body and voice gently, gradually raising the effort level as you go.

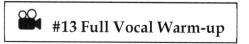

**#13 Full Vocal Warm-up**

**Full Warm-Up.** Allow 20 minutes

- Yawn and stretch, arms reaching up and out. Roll shoulders, shake legs, move face around.
- Find your feet hip-width apart, toes pointed straight ahead, weight spread evenly on the balls of the feet and the heels.
- Find softness in ankles and knees with a little bouncy "oingo, boingo."
- Bring awareness to the pelvic girdle and hips, and feel length in the lower spine.

- Sense your spine as it builds from the tailbone to your neck, starting with the tail bone, moving through your middle back, and building through your upper back to your neck. Feel the head floating on top of your spine.
- Feel the jaw hang loose, your tongue resting on the floor of the mouth.
- Move your right ankle in a circle; add an easy hum as you move the ankle. Move your left ankle in a circle, adding an easy hum.
- Move your hips in a large, loose circle. Add an easy "ah" in a comfortable part of your pitch range. Change directions. Feel the sound as the perfect accompaniment to the movement.
- Swing your arms like a child, twisting easily from side to side.
- Stretch the rib cage and intercostal muscles by extending one arm up and over and pat the rib cage with the other hand.
- Roll your shoulders with an "ee."
- Swing one arm like a windmill with an "oo." Then swing the other arm, also with an "oo."
- Drop the head forward. Let the chin rest on the chest and shake the head "no."
- Slowly lift the head. As you look right, exhale on "sh;" as you look left, inhale. Repeat slowly several times.
- Let chin drop to the chest and slowly roll down the spine. Release the head, shoulders, and knees. Breathe deeply into your lower back, feeling the lower back lift slightly toward the ceiling on each inhale. Sigh out several sighs of relief. Shake out some sound.
- Slowly roll up, one vertebra at a time. The head is the last to come up.
- T'ai chi (Chapter 6).
- Check in with abdominal release (Chapter 4).

- Wake up the recoil breath (Chapter 4).
- Bring awareness to the moment of readiness (Chapter 4).
- Hum starting on a lower note and slowly move the pitch of the hum up. Feeling the vibrations move from the chest, to the throat, to the mouth, to the forehead. (Chapter 6).
- Open vocal tract (Chapter 6): jaw, tongue and soft palate.
- Extend pitch range with the ng siren (Chapter 7).
- Recall optimum pitch with the Pringles tube (Chapter 7). Try a few lines of a speech using optimum pitch.
- Sing the text or do "Master Thespian" (Chapter 7).
- Ground and let the breath settle. Say your speech out loud from wherever the last exploration left you.
- Connect back with natural alignment and deep central breath. Think about the effect you want the speech to have on the audience in the form of an action verb and breathe it into your center. When you are connected to the real need, speak the text (Chapter 13).

## Hum Through (allow 5 minutes)

Humming though body parts is an efficient way to warm up if time is limited and the space you are in doesn't permit fully sounding.

- Put a hum in your ankles as you circle each.
- Put a hum in your hips as you circle them.
- Put a hum in your waist as you swing from side to side.
- Put a hum in your shoulders as you roll them backwards and forwards.
- Put a hum in each arm as you swing it full circle.
- Put a hum in your head as you look gently to the right and to the left.

- Put a hum in your head as you circle it gently.
- Put a hum in your face and move it around.
- Chew a hum.
- Hum through your pitch range from easy low notes, through your mid-range, to easy upper notes.
- Move a vibrant, juicy hum through your whole body, moving the body easily with the sound.

**T'ai Chi** and **The Archer** done in sequence provide a short but effective way to focus, connect to breath, warm up the voice and open pitch range.

To end the warm-up sing, dance, own the words, physicalize nouns and verbs or use "Pitch Absurd" to get the body and voice integrated.

## Forming Habits to Encourage Daily Practice

In this book I have given you a great deal of information about a range of topics that circle around voice: presence, confidence, owning the room, freeing the voice, body language, compelling presentations, leadership voice, running for office and vocal health. I have laid out a process that will yield lasting results. There is no substitute for practice. This work can be life changing, as it has been for hundreds of former students and clients. Not only that, but the work is endlessly invigorating. It need not be just a means to an end but an important part of your life.

I encourage you to dedicate time every day, perhaps linking your vocal warm-up to an already established habit. I do "voice yoga" at the end of my morning workout. If you don't already have a time set aside for personal care, think about what you can let go of to create time and space for this. How many times each day do you use your voice and how much rides on your ability to communicate effectively? Isn't it worth 10-15 minutes out of your day to insure that your voice is as good as it can be?

I want to leave you with this thought: women have never been in a better position to change the world. It is truly our time. Women who speak well are going to be powerful healing agents in the months and years to come. Use your authentic, strong and confident voice to lead from wherever you are – our combined sound will shatter inequities, barriers and glass ceilings. We can create success for ourselves, our communities, and our nation. Breathe deeply and speak from your heart each and every day.

**Final Reflective Journal:** What are the lessons or exercises presented in this book which have had the most impact on you? What changes have you noticed in your own voice? What are you more aware of in the communication style of others? How are you going to incorporate this practice into your life? What are your goals for moving forward in your vocal and physical communication?

_____
_____
_____
_____
_____
_____
_____
_____

# "Voices from the Field" Bios

**Teri Aulph** entered the corporate world in the middle of her career and within three years she rose to the level of executive in various Fortune 500 companies. Now as an author, speaker and business consultant for Fortune 500 companies around the globe, she helps companies capitalize on their biggest asset: their people - talent management and business solutions. She is also Senior Vice President and Chief Human Resources Officer for Tulsa Federal Credit Union.

**Angela Byers**, as the Founder and CEO of Byers Creative, started her company in a spare bedroom and built it into what it is today: an industry-leading, full-service agency specializing in branding and marketing solutions. Because of her strong leadership and success, she was named the "Woman of Distinction" by Tulsa Business and Legal news in 2015, the "Small Business Person of the Year" by the Tulsa Chamber in 2014, and the "John Hartman Professional of the Year" by IABC Tulsa in 2015. Angela is also a dedicated servant to her community and participates in numerous organizations, including the Executive Women's Forum (EWF), the Tulsa Small Business Connection (TSBC), the International Association of Business Communicators (IABC) and the Oklahoma Ethics Consortium.

**Felicia Collins Correia** served in non-profit executive leadership for over 25 years as CEO of Domestic Violence Interventions Services/Call Rape and the YWCA Tulsa. She oversaw two successful non-profit mergers and was instrumental in creating systemic change with Tulsa Law Enforcement (Police, Sheriff and District Attorney) and with the

Judiciary for which she received numerous awards in recognition of this work. She is now a consultant specializing in professionalizing non-profits, analyzing organizational and infrastructure gaps, and transforming staff and organizational culture.

**Cecilie Croissant** is a licensed professional counselor (LPC) and an ordained minister. She has pastored three churches, traveled to 35 countries for speaking engagements, and also served as the Director for the School of Worship Program at Victory Bible College for 10 years. Cecilie is an accomplished musician and worship leader, and has written study materials used in Bible Schools in the US, Peru, and Russia. She is the owner of Path of Hope Counseling, in Owasso, OK and is an adjunct professor at Southern Nazarene University.

**Aurora Gregory** is marketer, author and speaker. Some of the biggest brands in business have worked with her to get their message right, create communications programs that connect with target audiences, and set marketing strategies that deliver results. Aurora has received accolades as a communications trainer, helping those with something to say develop skills to deliver their most important messages to customers, media, and presentation audiences. She has years of experience in leading speaker's bureau programs that have placed hundreds of speakers at local, national, and international conferences. And she's passionate about coaching entrepreneurs on how to build meaningful connections with their customers so they can grow their businesses.

**Anna Fearheiley** is a Location Manager with iD Tech Camps, where she oversees technology education programs throughout New England. Her work includes training and coaching staff, interacting with students and parents, and speaking at recruiting and marketing events. In addition, Anna is the Associate Producer for Sanguine Theatre Company, a non-profit organization in New York City focused on new plays. She is a University of Oklahoma graduate and one of Rena Cook's former students and assistants.

**Kendra Horn** is currently running for US House of Representatives District # 5 in Oklahoma. Her career has taken her from Washington, DC to Colorado and California before returning to Oklahoma to make a difference in her home state. She is the Executive Director of Women Lead Oklahoma, a nonprofit dedicated to women's empowerment, leadership, and civic engagement and is a professional mediator. Previously, she served as press secretary for Congressman Brad Carson, led government affairs and communications for the Space Foundation, and practiced law. She has also managed political campaigns and served as Executive Director for Sally's List, where she led a concerted effort to get more women to run for and serve in elected office in Oklahoma.

**Ellen McClure** is Associate Professor of French and History at the University of Illinois-Chicago, where she has also served as Head of the Department of French and Francophone Studies and is currently the Associate Director of the School of Literatures, Cultural Studies, and Linguistics. She has also been directing the university's program in Religious Studies. She is the author of *Sunspots and the Sun King: Sovereignty and Mediation in Seventeenth-Century France* and soon to be published *The Logic of Idolatry: Creation, Authorship, and the Will in Seventeenth-Century France*. In her spare time, she serves as an ordained Zen Buddhist lay teacher at the Zen Buddhist Temple in Chicago, Illinois.

**Diana Morgan** is a Certified Life Coach, Health Coach, Certified EFT (Emotional Freedom Technique) Practitioner and a Matrix Reimprinting Practitioner. Both EFT and Matrix Reimprinting are powerful techniques to help people release stuck patterns and traumas so that they can attain their goals and find peace and happiness. Diana is the founder of Alchemy of Change, LLC. Diana holds a Master's Degree in Counseling Psychology from Boston College and is a Certified Clinical Herbalist and Nutritionist. She is passionate about natural healing in all its forms. Diana is currently the President of her Toastmaster's Club. The primary aspiration in her career is to help people to be happy, healthy and to follow their dreams. www.msdianamorgan.com

**Cheena Pazzo** owns and operates a strategic marketing communications consulting business. Having worked both in large international and small business environments, she is adept at providing services scaled to meet the unique needs of her clients. She previously served as Chief Communications and Marketing Officer for St. John Health System, where she led internal and external communications, marketing, consumer outreach, public relations and call center operations. Formerly, she was Director of Public Relations for Level 3 Communications and Manager of Public Relations and Marketing for TV Guide. Her philosophies on teamwork, business and communications have been nationally published.

**Jessica Reading** is Content Experience Director at Microsoft and has worked variously as a French localization specialist, instructional designer, web site manager, writer, and team lead. From translating Excel's macro language into French to learning just enough Visual Basic to code an interactive tutorial to developing a creative brief on editorial voice for Xbox, her contributions have always had as their end goal increasing the customer's mastery of and delight with their tools. As Content Experience Director, she is managing the talented teams who write for Windows user experiences, including support chat bots, cool apps such as Paint 3D, and the Windows Tips app. Words and stories are also at the core of her activities outside of Microsoft. She co-produces the multi-disciplinary literary performance series Letters Aloud, which has toured throughout the western US.

**Kathy Taylor** is a tireless advocate and change agent for Tulsa. Elected Mayor of Tulsa, OK in 2006, she saw the city through the worst recession in 70 years. She is currently Chief of Economic Development in the Office of Tulsa's Mayor, GT Bynum. She has also served as Oklahoma Secretary of Commerce and Tourism as well as Chief of Education Strategy and Innovation. She serves on the Board of Directors of Sonic Industries, Chair of the Leadership Council for ImpactTulsa, and is a regional board member of Reading Partners. Through the Lobeck Taylor Family Foundation she works to stay at the forefront of innovation and is a collaborator in Tulsa's entrepreneurial ecosystem.

# End Notes

## Introduction

[1] Christine K. Jahnke, *The Well Spoken Women: Your Guide to Looking and Sounding your Best.* Amherst: Prometheus Books, 2011.

## Chapter 1

[1] Christine K. Jahnke, *The Well Spoken Women: Your Guide to Looking and Sounding your Best.* Amherst: Prometheus Books, 2011.

[2] Meribeth Dayme, *Presence, Confidence, and Personal Power.* Pennsauken: BookBaby, 2014.

[3] Carol Gilligan, *In a Different Voice.* Cambridge: Harvard University Press, 2009.

[4] Katty Kay and Claire Shipman, The Confidence Code: *The Science and Art of Self Assurance.* New York: HarperCollins, 2014.

[5] Joanna Barsh, Susie Cranston, and Geoffrey Lewis, *How Remarkable Women Lead: The Breakthrough Model for Work and Life.* New York: Crown Business, 2009.

[6] The terms bluff and denial are adapted from the work of Patsy Rodenburg in her book *The Actor Speaks*, published by Bloomsbury Methuen Drama.

[7] Adam Bryant, "Knowing, as a Leader, When to let Go." *Wall Street Journal*, April 23, 2017.

## Chapter 2

[1] Christine K. Jahnke, *The Well Spoken Women: Your Guide to Looking and Sounding your Best.* Amherst: Prometheus Books, 2011.

[2] Meribeth Dayme, *Presence, Confidence and Personal Power.* Pennsauken: BookBaby, 2012.

## Chapter 3
[1] Sheryl Sandberg, *Lean In: Women, Work, and the Will to Lead.* New York: Knopf, 2013.

## Chapter 4
[1] Dennis Lewis, *The Tao of Natural Breathing.* San Francisco: Mountain Wind Publishing, 1997.

[2] David Carey, "The Responsive Breath," in *Breath in Action: The Art of Breath in Vocal and Holistic Practice.* Eds. Jane Boston and Rena Cook, London: Jessica Kingsley Publishers, 2009.

[3] "Breathing the Space" and Building Capacity are found in Patsy Rodenburg's book *The Actor Speaks* published by Bloomsbury Methuen Drama.

## Chapter 5

[1] Katty Kay and Claire Shipman, *The Confidence Code: The Science and Art of Self-Assurance.* New York: HarperCollins, 2014.

[2] Chelsea Handler, "What, Me Worry?" *InSTYLE Magazine*, June 2017.

[3] Maribeth Dayme, *Presence, Confidence and Personal Power.* Pennsauken: BookBaby, 2012.

4 Katty Kay and Claire Shipman, *The Confidence Code: The Science and Art of Self-Assurance.* New York: HarperCollins, 2014.

5 Ibid.

6 Andrew Weil, Breath: *The Master Key to Self Healing.* Watertown: Thorne Communications, Inc., 1999.

7 Sylvia Ann Hewlett, *Executive Presence: The Missing Link Between Merit and Success.* New York: HarperCollins, 2014.

## Chapter 6

1 Sylvia Ann Hewlett, *Executive Presence: The Missing Link Between Merit and Success.* New York: HarperCollins, 2014.

## Chapter 7

1 Sylvia Ann Hewlett, *Executive Presence: The Missing Link Between Merit and Success.* New York: HarperCollins, 2014.

2 Katty Kay, and Claire Shipman, *The Confidence Code: The Science and Art of Self Assurance.* New York: HarperCollins, 2014.

## Chapter 8

1 Kristi Hedges, *The Power of Executive Presence: Unlock Your Potential to Influence and Engage Others.* New York: AMACOM, 2012.

2 Katty Kay and Claire Shipman, *The Confidence Code: The Science and Art of Self Assurance.* New York: HarperCollins, 2014.

## Chapter 9

[1] Linda Hartley, *Wisdom of the Body Moving*. Berkeley: North Atlantic Books, 1995.

[2] Julian Fast, *Body Language*. New York: Pocket Books, 1972.

[3] Meribeth Dayme, *Presence, Confidence, and Personal Power.* Pennsauken: BookBaby, 2012.

[4] Google. "Why Michelle Obama is a Great Speaker." Accessed May 1, 2017. http://www.stalwartcom.com/blog/why-michelle-obama-is-a-great-speaker/

[5] Kristi Hedges, *The Power of Executive Presence: Unlock Your Potential to Influence and Engage Others*. New York: AMACOM, 2012.

## Chapter 10

[1] Natalie Goldberg, *Living the Writer's Life*. New York: Open Road Media, 2011.

## Chapter 11

[1] Steve Brown, *How to Talk So People Will Listen*. Grand Rapids: Baker Books, 1993.

## Chapter 12

[1] Caroline Goyder, *Gravitas: Communicate With Confidence, Influence and Authority.* London: Random House, 2014.

## Chapter 13

[1] Katty Kay and Claire Shipman, *The Confidence Code: The Science and the Art of Self Assurance.* New York: HarperCollins, 2014.

[2] Saraya Chemaly, "Women in Politics: Why We Need More Women in Office," blog post 3/1/12

[3] Google. "Gender, Women and Democracy," National Democratic Institute. <u>Accessed May 25, 2017.</u> <u>https://www.ndi.org/what-we-do/gender-women-and-democracy</u>

[4] Patsy Rodenburg, *The Actor Speaks.* New York: Palgrave MacMillan, 2002.

[5] David Carey and Rebecca Clark-Cary, *Verbal Arts Workbook.* London: Methuen Drama, 2010.

[6] "Pipeline to Politics," Conference presented by the Carl Albert Congressional Research and Studies Center: Women's Leadership Initiative and The Oklahoma Women's Coalition, January 28, 2017.

## Chapter 14

[1] Kate DaVore and Starr Cookman, *The Voice Book: Caring For, Protecting, and Improving Your Voice*. Chicago: Chicago Review Press.

[2] Joanna Cazden is my "go to" Speech Pathologist. Her book *Everyday Voice Care* is an excellent resource.

## Chapter 15

[1] Kristi Hedges, *The Power of Presence: Unlock Your Potential to Influence and Engage Others*. New York: AMACOM, 2012.

# Index

# More of What readers are saying about Empower your Voice

"Rena is a joy to watch in action and read, in her speeches, training sessions and writing. Her skill set and natural teaching ability make it easy to internalize and follow the steps she sets forth to allow you to find your true voice and confidence when communicating with others. I have benefited greatly from these lessons in my own business. Her dedication to helping women achieve success and recognize their worth in both business and their personal lives is a pleasure to witness. No matter your industry or background, you will benefit from the knowledge she shares in this book."
　　-Shannon Bisel, Real Estate Professional

*Empower your Voice* is positive and encouraging - just as Rena is in person. I had read her other book *Voice and the Young Actor* and, though the topics are similar, the shift in focus to make those topics relevant to women's lives makes the material even more effective. I appreciated the expanded discussions of the importance of our physical posture, regular voice practice, and self-care. I love the pencil illustrations and the photos. I recommend the book to any professional women interested in improving their voices."
　　-Jan Dodson, Geophysicist, STAR Geophysics

"As an actor/director/theatre voice teacher and a voice professional herself, Rena shares her insights, secrets and actionable tips for the business professional.
　　Useful and practical - not just ideas but usable techniques on how you can shift your voice to claim more power. It's not a quick fix but it is a real process and Rena will guide you."
　　-Hilary Blair, Co-founder and CEO, ARTiculate: Real&Clear

CPSIA information can be obtained
at www.ICGtesting.com
Printed in the USA
LVHW05s0954140418
573188LV00003BA/7/P